THE MEDICAL HISTORY
OF THE REFORMERS

MARTIN LUTHER

JOHN CALVIN

JOHN KNOX

by

JOHN WILKINSON
B.D., M.D., F.R.C.P.

THE HANDSEL PRESS LTD
Edinburgh

Published in 2001 by
The Handsel Press
58 Frederick St, Edinburgh

© John Wilkinson 2001

British Library Cataloguing in Publication Data:
A catalogue record for this publication
is available from the British Library
ISBN   1 871828 60 0

Typeset in 11 pt. Garamond

Cover by Junction Design

Thanks are expressed to the Drummond Trust,
3 Pitt Terrace, Stirling,
to the Hope Trust and others
for assistance with the costs of this publication

CONTENTS

ACKNOWLEDGEMENTS

The three chapters which form the bulk of this book were originally published in the Proceedings of the Royal College of Physicians of Edinburgh. These articles have now been completely revised and much expanded. They are studies of an area of joint medical and Church history which has been neglected in the past. Because of the international interest which was shown in them when they were first published, they are now made available in one volume. The author is grateful to Dr Antony Busuttil, Regius Professor of Forensic Medicine in the University of Edinburgh, and the current Editor of the Proceedings, for permission to publish them in this form.

Thanks are also expressed to New College Library for permission to reproduce the Contemporary Portraits of the Reformers of Religion and Letters - facsimile reproductions of the portraits in Beza's 'Icones' (1580) and in Goulard's edition (1581) with Introduction and Biographies by C.G. McCrie D.D. (London, Religious Tract Society 1909).

FOREWORD

Visitors to Geneva with any interest in church history are sure to make their way to the Reformation Wall. This long tableau depicts John Calvin, the sixteenth-century Reformer who more than anyone else made Geneva into a city of European importance, flanked on either side by other leading Protestant theologians and churchmen of that age of reform. Their exalted significance is inescapably suggested by their height in the sculpture, with Calvin in the middle head and shoulders above his colleagues. His exaggerated stature leaves the viewer in no doubt about his towering eminence in the Reformation movement, at least in the mind of the sculptor and the city fathers. This portrayal of John Calvin as almost a superhuman figure (his successor, Theodore Beza, described him as of moderate height) is typical of the idealisation to which heroes and heroines of the past have always been subjected. The statue*of John Knox in the quadrangle of New College, Edinburgh, is not so gigantic as Geneva's Calvin, but is no less triumphalist and larger than life. But idealised portraits of the Protestant Reformers are not restricted to the plastic or visual arts. Theologians and historians have displayed boundless ingenuity in presenting them as human beings marked not so much by that virtuosity of fallibility and wickedness they themselves so insistently ascribed to all humankind as by almost unerring soundness of mind and rectitude of life.

Dr John Wilkinson's studies of the medical histories of three of the most influential Reformers make an important contribution to cutting them down to size. His expertise in both medicine and theology is here joined by an historical sensibility. Together they give his investigations a clinical objectivity concerned above all to inform the reader just how far short Luther, Calvin and Knox fell of enjoying full physical well-being. They furnish a more secure basis for attempting that more difficult task of analysing their emotional or psychological histories. Writers have not been hesitant to advance bold exercises in psychohistory, chiefly on Luther but also on Calvin and Knox. But these must remain to some degree speculative unless anchored in a scientific appreciation of their bodily fortunes rendered by a physician. On an even more fundamental level, these medical histories are healthy grist for the biographers' mills. Martin Luther has been well served by modern lives both scholarly and attractively written. The same cannot be said with equal confidence of Knox (the best monograph, by Pierre Janton in 1967, was never translated from the French) and even less of Calvin. The human Calvin has proved elusive to the historian. Far less autobiographical than Luther and Knox, but surely no less self-revelatory to the discerning scrutineer of his vast body of writings, the Frenchman from Picardy who chaired the Company of Pastors in Reformation Geneva is certainly better known now that the tale of his afflicted existence *in corpore insano* is more precisely told.

What strikes me in reading these histories is in the first place how mundane were these Reformers' frailties. Gout may be less often encountered today, but constipation, kidney stone, bronchitis, pneumonia – how pathetically run-of-the-mill appear the chronic complaints of these extraordinary men. The prodigious dimension of their achievements is indirectly the second impression I take away from digesting these diagnoses. Knowing the many and varied illnesses from which John Calvin suffered for so much of his Genevan career merely deepens one's almost awed appreciation of how much he got done. If these Reformers are models for emulation, it is not as plaster saints but as human beings who shared in the vulnerabilities of flesh and blood, as also of mind and spirit, more intensely than most of us moderns. Dare we even say that, like Jesus Christ their Lord, such perfection as they attained came not only despite but actually through their physical sufferings?

There are, after all, few things more elemental to human life than health of body. John Wilkinson's researches thus touch the core of these Reformers' being. They help us forward in the task of seeing them whole at this historical distance. The three of them can ask nothing higher than that of their modern-day interpreters.

David F. Wright
Prof. of Patristic and Reformed History
New College, Edinburgh

MARTIN LUTHER.

JOHN CALVIN.

JOHN KNOX.

INTRODUCTION

A priest sees people at their best,
A lawyer at their worst,
but a doctor sees them as they really are.

If this saying is true then it means that a knowledge of a person's medical history is very relevant to the understanding of their character and life, and to the assessment of their behaviour and achievement. The importance of the medical history of a person has been recognised in recent years with the emergence of what is termed *psychohistory* or *psychobiography*. As these terms imply, the interest in the studies which they describe is psychological or psychoanalytical rather than strictly medical.

However, in the three studies of the medical histories of the Reformers contained in this present volume, we are concerned with the broader aspects of their experience of health and disease, and not merely the psychological.

It is surprising to find that these broader aspects have received relatively little attention in the immense amount of literature which has grown up around the person and work of the three Reformers whose medical history forms our subject. Part of the reason for this in the case of Calvin and Knox is their own reluctance to speak about themselves. Even though Luther is much less reluctant to speak about himself, he has not left many details of his medical history.

A recent literature search found thirteen articles on the medical history of Luther, but only one on Calvin and none at all on Knox. Of the articles on Luther, eight were in German, two in English and one each in Hungarian, Norwegian and Spanish, an indication of a continuing international interest in the medical history of Luther.

This interest in Luther's medical history began to appear towards the end of last century when a book was published on the subject in 1881 in Leipzig by the German parasitologist, G.F.H. Kürchenmeister with the title *Dr Martin Luthers Krankengeschichte* (Dr Martin Luther's Medical History). In spite of its age, this book is still regarded as the best and most comprehensive survey. A more recent volume is by Dr William Ebstein, published in Stuttgart in 1908 with a similar title. Ebstein was professor of medicine at the University of Göttingen. In 1884 he reported his success with the experimental production of urinary calculi and this may explain his interest in Luther's medical history, in which urinary calculi played so important a part. However, the works of both these medical men are over ninety years old, were written in German and have never been translated into English. Also, our knowledge and understanding of the natural history of the diseases from which Luther suffered have greatly increased since the books were written and many of their comments would not be acceptable today. The most interesting recent publication on the subject which has appeared in English is the report of a discussion by a panel of physicians on Luther's medical history which appeared in *Chicago Medicine* in February 1966.

By contrast, very little has been published on the medical history of John Calvin. There are a number of incidental references to Calvin's health in the contemporary biographies of his colleagues Theodore Beza and Nicolas Colladon, but the most comprehensive survey available is that of Emile Doumergue, who was the professor of Church history in the Faculty of Theology at Montauban in the south of France. Over the years 1899 to 1927 he published a monumental study of the life and times of Calvin in seven large volumes written in French. In his third volume (published in 1905) he devoted a chapter of seventeen pages to the illnesses of Calvin. In writing this chapter he had the assistance of Dr Leon Gautier, a Swiss medical historian of Geneva. In 1958, Jean Cadier of the Faculty of Theology of Montpellier University, another of Calvin's biographers, published a useful short study in French of the illnesses from which Calvin suffered, based on a review of his letters. More recently, Dr Charles Cooke, a physician of Richmond, Virginia contributed an article of ten pages on Calvin's illnesses to a symposium devoted to Calvin and published in America in 1990.

In the case of John Knox, we have found no published study of his medical history. There are references to illness scattered throughout his writings, and mentioned by his biographers, but these are rare and scanty. For instance, we know from his own writings that Knox suffered numerous attacks of fever, but these are rarely mentioned in the standard biographies of the Reformer.

The result is that any study of the medical history of the three Reformers must go back to their own writings, and in the case of Luther also to his own sayings in the famous *Table Talk* which was recorded by his students at mealtimes in his home. These primary sources shed an interesting light on the practice of medicine and the diseases which were prevalent in sixteenth-century Europe, together with their diagnosis and treatment.

This century, to which all three of our three Reformers belonged, was the great century of change and progress in the history of Europe.

It formed a distinct watershed between the medieval and the modern worlds. The Reformers themselves were, of course, involved in the religious change in this century which we now call the Reformation, but change affected other areas of life and thought too, including those of medical thought and practice. Some of these are reflected in their medical histories as we shall see in more detail in the chapters which follow.

One of these changes was the emergence and organisation of the medical profession. Indeed, it was in the sixteenth century that physicians first began to organise themselves into professional associations concerned with the standards of medical practice and the basis on which practitioners should be recognised as competent to practice.

Each of the three Reformers had medical attendants in whose competence they appear to have had great confidence. We know most about those who attended Luther when he was ill. His favourite personal physician was Dr Georg Sturtz of Erfurt. He it was whom Luther specially summoned to his bedside when he had his most severe attack of the stone at Schmalkalden in Hesse in 1537. Luther was there to attend a conference of the Protestant princes and theologians and each prince had with him his own Court physician who was available to advise on Luther's treatment, but Luther demanded that Dr Sturtz be sent for. On other occasions, Luther was treated by the physicians on the staff of the various German Courts of the Protestant states. One who is specially mentioned is Dr Kaspar Lindemann, a nephew of Luther's wife, who was the personal physician to the Elector of Saxony and later the Professor of Medicine at Wittenberg University. He was also treated by Dr Matthaeus Ratzeberger, the Court physician of the Counts of Mansfeld, which was Luther's native district. After Luther's death, Dr Ratzeberger wrote a short biography of the Reformer which, however, is not regarded as very reliable.

Two doctors are named as attending Calvin and his wife in Geneva. The first was Dr Benedict Textor who attended Calvin's wife in her confinement and continued to look after both of them until he died about 1556. He was succeeded by Dr Philibert Sarrazin who was even more eminent in his profession than his predecessor. Four months before Calvin died, Sarrazin sought specialist advice about his treatment from the physicians of the Medical Faculty of Montpellier University in the south of France, which at that time was one of the leading medical centres in Europe.

In the case of Knox, the only doctor mentioned is a Dr Preston who was called in by his friends two weeks before his death. Since he appears to have been known to Knox and his friends, it is probable that he had attended Knox on previous occasions during Knox's residence in Edinburgh.

All three Reformers were ready to follow medical advice, although Luther cannot have been an easy patient for he was often quite forthright in his opinion about his doctors, apparently regarding them as a necessary evil and calling that man wretched who had to rely on their help. Nevertheless, he said he was always careful to obey their instructions lest they blame him for not looking after his health, for he accepted that the physician is God's mender of the body as the theologian is the mender of the soul.

There were several diseases from which all three of our Reformers suffered, which must therefore have been common in their time. Thus, for instance, we read of attacks of gout, urinary calculi and fevers or agues of various kinds, many of which were probably malarial in origin. The use of the term 'marsh ague' to describe some of these fevers arose from the observation that fevers were common near marshlands, an association which was only explained when the role of marsh-breeding mosquitoes in the malaria cycle was discovered in the nineteenth century. Also there are references to various diseases with which they had contact, such as measles, bacillary dysentery, bubonic plague and the mysterious English Sweating Sickness. The most feared was bubonic plague of which there have been three pandemics in recorded history, the second of which affected Europe at the time of the Reformation and caused the deaths of many of Luther's colleagues and friends. This pandemic was originally spoken of as *The Great Pestilence*, and then in the early nineteenth century it was called *The Black Death* because of the haemorrhages which often appeared in the skin of victims of the the disease.

For the first forty years of his life, Luther does not appear to have suffered from any significant illness. Even the severe discipline of his monastic life, made yet more severe by his own search after spiritual peace by long prayer vigils and rigorous fasting, seems to have produced no serious permanent damage to his health.

Calvin, on the other hand, began to experience poor health as a student. Theodore Beza, his earliest biographer, attributes the early onset of Calvin's ill health to his intense application to study which constantly led him to go without food and sleep.

By contrast, Knox was normal and healthy until he was imprisoned by the French and consigned to the galleys as a galley slave. At one point during this period he became so ill that his life was in danger. However, he survived this experience, and although he may never have really recovered his normal state of health, he went on to carry a tremendous burden of work and responsibility until he died a worn-out and exhausted man at the age of fifty-seven.

There are vivid descriptions of the clinical features of various diseases in the writings of all three Reformers. Luther tells us about his troublesome experience of constipation, calling it his 'vexatious handicap'. Both Luther and Calvin speak of haemorrhoids which made horse-riding difficult. This was a great disability in an age when a common means of travel was on horseback. All three of the Reformers suffered from urinary calculi, popularly called 'the stone' or 'gravel'. Calvin gives us a very dramatic description of attacks of renal colic with their excruciating and disabling episodes of pain and prostration, produced by the body in its attempts to expel the stones which had formed in the kidney. All three also suffered from gout which explains the origin of their urinary calculi.

As we shall see in some detail in the following chapters, it is possible to diagnose with some degree of probability the diseases from which our Reformers died. Luther appears to have developed hypertensive heart disease in later life and had several 'heart attacks' until he finally died of myocardial infarction. Calvin provides a dramatic picture of the occurrence and clinical effects of pulmonary tuberculosis, a disease from which he ultimately died. The cause of Knox's death was less specific and appears to have been extreme physical exhaustion which left him open to an attack of a fatal lower respiratory infection.

We learn something too about the diagnostic methods of medicine in the sixteenth century, although it was true that physicians of this time attempted too much diagnosis on the basis of too little knowledge. Luther appears to have been in the habit of feeling his own pulse. On one occasion he recognised that it was irregular, but was relieved to find that his physician regarded the irregularity as of no significance. He also refers to urinoscopy or 'water-casting' as a method of diagnosis on two occasions, on one of which his physician used it to exclude apoplexy. During Calvin's long illness, his physicians were able to discover that his spleen was enlarged, a condition which they explained in terms of the then current humoral theory of disease which traced the cause of splenic enlargement to the liver.

There are several descriptions of the treatment of disease. The most memorable of these is the attempt to relieve the eight-day retention of urine which Luther suffered at an important conference in the small German town of Schmalkalden which we have already mentioned. This town was small and had neither a physician nor an apothecary. Fortunately there were numerous physicians attending the princes who were at the conference and we are given some indication of what went on in the various medical consultations they held over their patient. They are described in such detail that we can quite imagine ourselves at the bedside, as the various decisions about treatment were made and then carried out.

The methods and remedies of folk medicine were not infrequently used by Luther. On one occasion he claimed to be successful in treating an attack of angina pectoris with a watery extract of the blessed thistle (*Aqua cardui benedicti*). One source of the folk remedies he used was the Faecal Pharmacopoeia, which contained prescriptions compounded with faeces from various sources. Pig faeces were used as well as horse faeces and even human faeces. The latter kind was recommended for the treatment of wounds.

In the three chapters which follow, the medical histories of the three reformers Martin Luther, John Calvin and John Knox are set out and examined along the traditional lines laid down for medical history-taking and the systematic examination of the sick person. As far as is possible, the results of these two basic medical procedures are given in the words of the sick person concerned, as recorded in their own writings or the observations of others with whom they had to do. The list of references which follow each chapter provides the details of the sources from which these descriptions or observations are taken.

Chapter 1

THE MEDICAL HISTORY OF MARTIN LUTHER

Martin Luther was 'a prodigious man in a prodigious age, a hero in a time of heroes'.[1] It is not surprising, therefore, that the details and significance of his life and work have given rise to a vast literature over the five centuries which have elapsed since his birth. Very little of this literature, however, has been concerned with his medical history.

The Sources

Luther himself had promised his friends that he would write an autobiography but poor health and overwork prevented him from providing more than the short autobiographical fragment of nine pages which introduced the 1545 Latin edition of his works.[2] His father too had planned to write a biographical memoir of his famous son, but died before he could do so.[3] The first formal biography was written in Latin in 1546 by his close friend and colleague Philip Melanchthon, but this occupies only eight pages.[4] Several other biographies appeared later but these too were short and provided few details of his medical history.[5]

However, there are two other sources of information. One consists of the numerous letters Luther wrote to his wife, his friends and a large number of other correspondents. Many of these letters were not preserved, but some 2,600 have survived, written in either German or Latin. In many cases, the originals of these letters have not survived and now exist only as copies, so that we cannot always be completely certain of what he wrote. There are even cases in which conflicting copies of the same letter exist. Fortunately for our present purpose, there are numerous references to his state of health in those letters which have been preserved.

The other source is the famous *Table Talk (Tischreden* or *Colloquia Mensalia)* of Luther. This consists of Luther's informal dinner-table comments and reminiscences which were made to the students and others who shared his mealtimes. These comments were recorded in shorthand during each meal or written up afterwards by a succession of twelve of Luther's students who, in accordance with the custom followed at the University of Wittenberg, were boarders in the home of their professor. These records were begun in 1531 and continued until 1546, the year of his death. However, they must be treated with some caution as they are second-hand and their reliability depends on the accuracy of Luther's recollection of what in some cases were long-past events, together with the care with which they were recorded and edited.

Family History

The ancestors of Martin Luther were small landowners who had lived for generations in the small village of Möhra (Moortown) in Thuringian Saxony in eastern Germany, about eight miles south of Eisenach. The village housed only sixty or seventy families but was not large enough to have a parish priest or church of its own. Here Luther's grandfather, Heine Luder (as the family name was probably spelled originally) owned considerable property and all the Luther families during Martin's lifetime lived there in relatively comfortable circumstances, owning the fields they tilled and the houses in which they lived.[6] Martin's father, Hans Luther, was the eldest of four sons and when their father died, Hans had to set out to make his own fortune in the world in accordance with the local Thuringian law governing family inheritance. This law did not recognise the principle of primogeniture nor the alternative practice of dividing the family farm between all the sons. According to the law it was the youngest son who inherited the house and farm and the others had to move out to allow him to do so.

Before he left Möhra, Hans married Margaret (Greta) Lindemann who was a member of a well-established middle-class burgher family in the town of Eisenach, which lay about fifteen miles to the north of Möhra and was one of the principal towns of Thuringia. The date and details of the marriage ceremony are unknown. The status of his wife's family is illustrated by the fact that several members of it became university graduates and became prominent members of their professions and of society. Her nephew Johannes Lindemann became professor of law at Leipzig University. His brother Kaspar studied medicine at Leipzig, Frankfurt-on-Oder and Bologna and became personal physician to the Elector of Saxony. He treated Martin Luther on several occasions and for the last four years of his life (1532-1536) he was professor of medicine at Wittenberg University.[7]

After his marriage, Hans moved with his wife from Möhra in search of new employment. They went to the small town of Eisleben, a distance of about eighty miles to the north, where her eldest brother was already settled. Eisleben was in the county of Mansfeld and had a population of about four thousand people. The Eisleben-Mansfeld area of the Harz mountains had recently become one of the important copper mining centres of Germany and so from being a farmer, Hans became a copper-miner.[8]

Between 11pm and midnight on Monday, 10 November 1483, Margaret Luther was delivered of her firstborn child - a son.[9] We know the hour of the birth because she told Luther's friend and colleague at Wittenberg, Philip Melanchthon, many years later how she heard the clock strike twelve midnight as she lay in bed after the delivery was over.[10] Next day, he was baptised by Bartholomew Rennebecher, the parish priest, in the lower tower room of the nearby parish Church of St Peter, which was then in the process of construction.[11] Since that day was the feast of St Martin of Tours, the child was called Martin. Martin was the eldest of seven children who were eventually born to the Luthers. He had three brothers and three sisters, of whom only one brother (called Jacob or James) and three sisters reached adulthood. His other two brothers died of plague in 1505, about the same time that he entered the monastery at Erfurt.

At first, Hans does not appear to have been successful in obtaining satisfactory employment in Eisleben and so, about six months after Martin was born, he and his young family moved from Eisleben to the county town of Mansfeld about six miles away. This town was about the same size as Eisleben, but was more in the centre of the copper-mining region. To begin with, the family found themselves in more modest circumstances than those to which they had been accustomed. Soon, however, Hans prospered and became a smeltermaster by leasing three copper-smelters from their owners, the Counts of Mansfeld, who had built them for leasing to local skilled workmen such as Hans. He soon gained the respect of other members of the community and in 1491 he became one of the four community representatives elected to the Mansfeld town council. By 1511 he was part-owner of six copper-mines and two furnaces and had become in modern terms, 'an early small industrialist and capitalist'.[12] The substantial two-storey stone house which the family eventually purchased and occupied, stood at the lower end of the main street, but is not maintained in its original form today although Hans Luther's coat of arms of a hammer laid on a block of stone, still adorns the front door.[13]

Luther had been born into a society of practising Christian men and women, where every child was a living part of it and where the centre of its life, apart from the constant daily toil of its members, was the parish Church. His was a deeply pious and hard-working home and as one of his recent biographers has observed, 'there was character in Luther's parentage: uprightness, determination, integrity, ability and independence'.[14]

Little is known of the medical history of his parents. Martin's father died on 29 May 1530 after an illness which had lasted about four months, but whose nature is unknown. His mother died on 30 June in the following year. Luther was unable to attend the death-bed or funeral of either of his parents because his life was in too much danger at the time of their deaths. In a letter written when he heard the news of his father's death, he refers to him as 'that dear and gentle old man whose name I bear'.[15]

Education

Luther's father Hans had never attended school for there was no school in Möhra, and consequently he had never learned to read.[16] However, he was determined that Martin should receive what he had lacked.

When he was seven years old, Martin entered the local Latin school in Mansfeld.[17] This was a *Trivialschule* in which the curriculum was the medieval *Trivium* of grammar, logic and rhetoric which was considered as essential for all pupils who were seeking an advanced education. There were few books, for paper was expensive and so the pupils learned what was written on the classroom blackboard by the teacher. This they then copied on to their slates and learned by constant repetition.[18] School discipline was severe and pupils were often punished when they failed to repeat their grammatical lessons correctly. On one occasion, Luther tells us that he was thrashed fifteen times during the same morning in the Latin lesson for failing to decline and conjugate nouns and verbs, even though he had not yet been taught how to do either of these exercises.[19] Under this brutal regime, school-life became a martyrdom,[20] and examinations resembled trials for murder.[21]

About Easter 1497 when he was thirteen years old, Luther went to Magdeburg in accordance with the contemporary custom of 'the wandering scholar' who moved from school to school in search of instruction.[22] Magdeburg was on the River Elbe about forty miles north of Mansfeld. It was here that Luther attended the *Trivialschule* attached to the cathedral, which was run by the Brethren of the Common Life.[23] Luther also sang in the cathedral choir at Magdeburg for he was very musical and had a fine tenor voice, so much so that in later years he was called `the nightingale of Wittenberg' and showed himself to be a competent poet and composer as well as a theologian and reformer. On one occasion he claimed that music was second only to theology as a comfort to the human soul.[24]

A year later he went on to the old and famous parish Latin school of St George in Eisenach, the city which was the former residence of the Electors of Saxony. Here he stayed for four happy years in an atmosphere of warm friendship, musical company and active Church observance. He would later refer to Eisenach as 'my dear city (*meiner lieben Stadt*)'.[25] Here too he was able to enjoy contact with the relatives and friends of both his parents.[26] During his stay in Eisenach he lodged with Conrad and Ursula Cotta and took his meals with the family of Heinrich Schalbe, who all lived in the same house. Frau Cotta was the daughter of Heinrich Schalbe, who was mayor of Eisenach in 1495 and again in 1499.[27]

In May 1501, when he was not yet eighteen, Luther matriculated for the summer term at the University of Erfurt. Founded in 1392 by the burghers of the town, this institution was the oldest and most famous university in Germany in Luther's day and was attended by about two thousand students each year. In the matriculation register his name appears as *Martinus Ludher ex Mansfelt*. This is the first mention of him in any still-extant document.[28]

Here he joined the *bursa* or college of St George beside Lehmann's Bridge in the north-east area of the city, and became subject to the strict discipline and numerous regulations of college life. After three terms of the study of philosophy in the Faculty of Liberal Arts,[29] he graduated Bachelor of Arts on Michaelmas Day in September 1502, being placed thirtieth in a class of fifty-seven. Early in 1505 he obtained his Master of Arts degree and this time he was placed second in a list of seventeen candidates.[30]

In obedience to his father's wish that he should become a lawyer, a profession of honour and profit, Luther now changed to the Faculty of Law at Erfurt in May 1505. However, on Wednesday 2 July of that year he was caught in a severe thunderstorm near the village of Stotternheim as he returned to Erfurt from visiting his parents at Mansfeld. A thunderbolt struck the ground beside him and he fell down trembling with fear, and underwent a deep emotional and spiritual experience in the course of which he called on the aid of St Anne, the mother of the Virgin Mary and the patron saint of the miners of Saxony, and vowed to become a monk.[31]

Fifteen days later, in accordance with this vow and having sold all his books except his Plautus and Virgil which he took with him into the monastery,[32] Luther knocked on the great wooden door of the monastery of the Augustinian Eremites ('The Black Cloister'[33]) which was beside his own college of St George. When he was admitted, he asked the prior to enrol him in the novitiate of that Order.[34] With this apparently inauspicious step he entered upon the career that was to make him one of the outstanding figures in the history of modern Europe.[35]

He was now twenty-two years of age and he spent the next five years away from public life in the monastery at Erfurt, during which he fulfilled the requirements of his novitiate and proceeded through the orders of sub-deacon, deacon and priest. He was ordained a priest in the cathedral at Erfurt on 3 April 1507 and celebrated his first festive Mass on Cantate Sunday, 2 May, which his father and twenty of his relatives and friends from Mansfeld attended.

At the beginning of the winter term in October 1508, he was appointed to the chair of moral philosophy at the University of Wittenberg, but was recalled to Erfurt after a year. Two years later, in the summer of 1511, he was again transferred to Wittenberg to complete his theological studies and obtain his doctorate in theology there, and then to occupy the chair of biblical theology in succession to his friend and mentor Johann von Staupitz, the vicar-general of the German Augustinians. He obtained his doctorate on 19 October 1512 and joined the university teaching staff at the beginning of the academic year in 1513. At that time there were only about three hundred students at the university, although there were twenty-two professors.[36] In August 1518, Philip Melanchthon came from Tübingen to become the first professor of Greek at Wittenberg at the early age of twenty-one. It was under the influence of Luther and Melanchthon that Wittenberg became the first European university to adopt the principles of the Reformation.

Wittenberg (The White Mountain) was the capital of Electoral Saxony, but it had no university until one was founded in July 1502 by the Emperor Maximilian I and Elector Frederick the Wise in order to rival the university of Leipzig in neighbouring Ducal Saxony, which had been founded in 1409. Although it was the electoral capital, Wittenberg was hardly a propitious site for a university, being a very small town with a total population of only two thousand people and only 356 rateable houses according to the town register in 1513. In Luther's time it is described as insignificant, unattractive and poor, its houses mainly built of mud with roofs thatched with straw and its streets filthy and uncared for.[37]

On this occasion, his transfer to Wittenberg was permanent and it was here that he was to spend the rest of his life as professor of biblical theology, apart from a few rare visits to the world outside. As events turned out, he did not die in Wittenberg, but in Eisleben his birthplace. However, at the insistence of the Elector John Frederick, his body was brought back to Wittenberg for burial in the Castle Church there.

Factors Relating to Luther's Health

There are a number of possible factors which are relevant to any discussion of Luther's health.

Poverty has often been suggested as a factor which affected Luther's health as he grew up, but it is probable that poverty was not a factor which affected Luther's health significantly, although in the past Luther's biographers have commonly described him as growing up in 'grinding, squalid poverty'.[38] It is now realised that Luther's parents both came from families which possessed property and never lacked the necessities of life, although Hans' position may not at first have been entirely free from economic anxiety and risk.[39] However, long before Martin left home, his father's hard work and thrift had improved their social and economic status and before their son was through high school at Eisenach they had been able to purchase a substantial house in the most desirable part of Mansfeld. There is no suggestion that the health of their children was affected by poverty. So far as Martin himself is concerned we have a contemporary account of his parents as small and short, while he far surpassed them in build and height, which does not suggest that he was brought up in poverty.[40]

The *second* factor is that of Luther's asceticism as a monk. During his time as a monk at Erfurt (1505-11), Luther gained a reputation for ascetic piety far beyond the walls of the monastery. He fasted for days at a time and night after night he went without sleep in his search for spiritual peace. In a letter written in 1518 describing this period of his life, Luther admits, 'I almost met my death by my fasting, abstinence and austerity in labour and clothing; by all this my body was terribly weakened and exhausted'.[41] He lost so much weight that even in 1519 when he attended the Leipzig Disputation after he had been eight years at Wittenberg (and already had begun to put on weight) he was described by Mosellanus as 'of middle height with a slender body worn out both by study and care, so that you can almost count his bones through his skin'.[42]

The *third* factor was the stress to which he was exposed once he had emerged as a leader in the events of the Reformation. All the forces which could be brought to bear on him by the Roman Church and the Emperor Charles V, its secular protector, sought to make him recant his opinions. At his famous appearance before the Imperial Diet at Worms in April 1521 he refused to recant and ended his speech of refusal with the memorable and immortal words, 'Here I stand; I can do no other. So help me God. Amen'.[43] The result of his refusal was that he was excommunicated by the Roman Church and outlawed by the Holy Roman Empire.

The *fourth* factor was the huge workload he had to carry. In Wittenberg he was professor, preacher and pastor to the university and the community. These duties alone constituted a full-time occupation. In addition he was leader and adviser to the whole Reformation movement in Germany and abroad. He wrote much of its its theological and polemical literature and conducted a voluminous correspondence. He has been described as 'the most prolific author Germany has ever produced'.[44] Nevertheless he regarded his lifelong full-time calling to be that of the exposition of the Bible to his students at Wittenberg, and as one author has put it, 'in between lectures, so to speak, he began the Protestant Reformation'.[45] The tremendous double workload which resulted from all this activity could not but affect his physical and mental health.

The *fifth* factor was Luther's robust Christian faith. He had sought such a faith in his years in the monastery at Erfurt but he had failed to find it. It was only after he took up his teaching duties as professor of biblical theology at Wittenberg that he found it. As he was preparing his lectures on the Psalms in the autumn of 1514,[46] he discovered for himself that righteousness in the sight of God was not something earned by good works, but was a gift of God's grace given in response to human faith. This realisation that 'the just shall live by faith' (Romans 1:17) is traditionally known as his 'Tower experience (*Turmstubenerlebnis*)' because it occurred whilst he was at work at his desk in his little room on the third storey of the tower of the monastery at Wittenberg, preparing one of his lectures on the Psalms.[47] In this experience which in theological terms would be described as his 'conversion', Luther said that he felt himself 'straightaway born again'.[48] It was this experience which formed the basis of Luther's deep and strong faith enabling him to face with courage and equanimity all the forces of men and the Devil, which assailed him during his life thereafter. It was this experience too which was enshrined in the great principle of human justification before God on the grounds of divine grace and human faith alone which was the principle on which the Protestant Reformation was founded.

Luther as a person

What we know of Luther's general appearance we owe to the casual remarks of his friends and enemies about him. He appears to have been of medium height and taller than both his parents. He had a well-proportioned body with strong shoulders, and he held himself very erect whilst he walked.[49] However, he became very thin during his time as a monk.

His facial appearance resembled that of his mother rather than that of his father. A number of authentic portraits of him still exist, all by his friend Lucas Cranach the elder except the death-bed sketch and etching which were made by Lucas Fortnagel of Halle. Cranach was an apothecary by vocation and lived in Wittenberg from 1505 to 1550, where he also served as court painter to the Elector of Saxony. He was the leading painter of Saxony in the sixteenth century, and first produced a woodcut and three etchings of Luther in 1520 and 1521. These were followed by six oil paintings of him in 1521, 1525, 1526, 1528, 1532, and 1537. These portraits by Cranach show him first with dark brown hair which by 1528 is beginning to turn grey. From a medical point of view, the interesting feature is the increasing fullness of his face which becomes markedly obese by the time of his death as appears from the death-bed sketch of Fortnagel.[50]

Many observers were struck by his eyes with their deep brown-black colour and their penetrating gaze. They compared them to the eyes of lions, eagles and falcons because they had a fiery, burning sparkle about them. When he preached from the pulpit it seemed to the congregation that he could look right through them and see everything that they had done during the previous week.[51]

All who heard him either as preacher or professor were impressed by his voice. 'It was clear, penetrating, and of pleasing timbre, which, added to its sonorous, baritone resonance, contributed much to his effectiveness as a public speaker'.[52] Acoustically, he found the Castle Church at Wittenberg difficult to speak in.

He had many other remarkable gifts which may be summarised as follows: a warm and magnetic personality, a phenomenal memory, an original and penetrating mind combined with a marked dramatic and musical ability, a sense of humour and a ready pen.[53] He was described by Mosellanus at the Leipzig Disputation in 1519 as 'a joker in society, vivacious and sure, always with a happy face no matter how hard his enemies press him'.[54]

We know very little of Luther's personal habits, particularly after his marriage to Katharine von Bora. During the first thirty-eight years of his life he was extremely thin because of his abstemiousness in diet and his austerity of life, but his wife provided a greater variety of food for him and encouraged him to eat it. The result of this improved diet and his increased interest in food was that he put on weight until his obesity became proverbial and Goethe two centuries or so later could describe an obese person as being 'as fat as Martin Luther'.[55]

Luther would not drink the water of Wittenberg, declaring it to be unsafe and deadly (*letifera*).[56] In common with many of his contemporaries he drank beer and wine instead of water for this reason. His wife brewed beer for the household and his friends often gave him substantial presents of wine. Some of his biographers have suggested that he was addicted to alcohol, but there is no evidence of any serious alcoholism in his case, although he did drink to excess on occasions.[57]

We have few details of his personal hygiene, but it is recorded that after they were married, his wife discovered that the straw mattress on his bed had not been properly shaken out for a whole year. It was rotting from the moisture of Luther's sweat, a state which Luther himself had not noticed as he fell exhausted into his bed night after night. His personal servant, Wolfgang Seberger, although faithful, was not noted for his diligence, nor his sense of order or cleanliness.[58]

Luther's Personality

From the time that Luther emerged as the leader of the Reformation in Germany many assessments of his personality have been made.

In recent years, attempts have been made by psychologists and psychiatrists interested in history to explain 'the Luther phenomenon' in psychological and psychiatric terms, but these attempts are rarely well-founded for the basic data are almost entirely lacking. One of Luther's recent biographers comments on these attempts as follows: 'Little is known about the relationship of the young Luther with his father, and even less about that with his mother. Yet repeated attempts have been made, principally from the side of the psychological disciplines, to explain Luther's personality and its development on the basis of these relationships'.[59]

The most influential book on this subject has been *Young Man Luther: A Study in Psychoanalysis and History* written by the American psychoanalyst Erik H Erikson.[60] Erikson describes what he regards as the three most significant experiences of Luther's life. These are the thunderstorm at Stotternheim in 1505; the 'fit in the choir' at Erfurt in 1507, and 'the Tower experience' at Wittenberg in 1514. There is no doubt of the importance of the first and third of these experiences, but Erikson overemphasises and overdramatises the second, which he admits is not even mentioned by Luther in his writings. It was an intense experience of spiritual conviction, a denial that he was possessed by a demon, and not a fit in the usual sense of the term, even though some authors have made the unlikely suggestion that it was an epileptic seizure. Erikson's reconstruction of Luther's spiritual experience has not escaped serious criticism from Luther scholars. For instance, Bainton writes of Erikson's attempt to use psychoanalysis to explain Luther's early years, as follows: 'My critique here is threefold. The first is that the evidence is scant, late and flimsy; the second, that the projections from childhood to adolescence and maturity are sometimes false, sometimes unnecessary, and sometimes implausible. The third is that the motives attributed to Luther are invalid'.[61] Bainton points out that the evidence on which Erikson largely builds his case consists of three sayings about the harshness of his parents and his teachers towards him in his youth, taken from Luther's *Table Talk* which includes over seven thousand of his sayings. These sayings were spoken when he was fifty years old, were recorded by students often in discordant versions, and were never seen by Luther himself. This means that they need to be treated with caution and critically assessed before they can be made the basis of any speculative interpretation.

We have already suggested that Luther had a strong and well-rounded personality, of which the most important aspect was his robust Christian faith. We may be able to trace the historical events of his life and recognise the sources of the stress and turbulence of his times and his own personal and social life. We may also be able to describe the psychological factors which may appear to have influenced the development of his personality according to our modern understanding of such factors. However, these historical events and psychological influences were but secondary factors in his development as a leader of the Reformation. They do not explain how Luther came to be what he was and came to do what he did in the cause of the reformation of the medieval Roman Church. Any real and adequate understanding of him and his work must be based, not primarily on historical or psychological considerations, but on the theological convictions which formed the basis of his faith and the consequences which these had in his life, his thought and actions.

During Luther's own lifetime and frequently since, it has been suggested that he suffered from some mental disorder. In the papal bull *Decet Romanum* of 3 January 1521, which excommunicated Luther from the Roman Church, Pope Leo X said that it gave him 'grievous sorrow and perplexity' to say that Luther was 'the slave of a depraved mind', although no evidence was produced for this diagnosis.[62]

The evidence which various authors have used to support a diagnosis of mental disorder in Luther's case comes from two main sources. The first is his own writings and his comments recorded in his *Table Talk* and the second is in the statements of his opponents. Neither of these sources can be regarded as providing reliable clinical evidence of mental disorder.

With regard to the evidence from Luther himself, Haile comments as follows:

> Luther spoke and wrote freely about his infirmities, often embarrassingly so. In a way typical of the age but also revealing of this openhearted man, he regularly begged for the prayers of his friends. The modern psychiatrist, nonplussed, quotes such passages as sure evidence of a pathological mental condition.

Haile goes on to say that these references by Luther to physical and mental sufferings must be read 'in sympathy with his character and in the spirit of their times, not our own'.[63]

The two most common disorders from which Luther is alleged to have suffered are those of a chronic alcoholism and a manic-depressive psychosis (a bipolar affective disorder).[64] There is no doubt that he drank beer and less commonly wine, for this was the custom of his time because of the uncertain purity of the water available for drinking. On occasions he drank them to excess, but there is no evidence of any serious alcoholism.[65] It is recorded, for instance, that 'when he lectured on Noah's drunkenness (Genesis 9:20-22), Luther thought that he himself should get drunk the night before, so that he could speak as an expert about this wickedness'.[66] Even if he were serious, this does not suggest that he was an habitual drunkard, familiar with the experience and symptoms of drunkenness.

He certainly experienced periodic episodes of depression, which is not surprising in view of the acute physical suffering he had to endure during his attacks of renal colic; the personal opposition to his reforms he had to face, and the constant threats to his life and liberty which were made by his opponents. As the British psychiatrist, Gaius Davies, points out, it is possible that there was a marked physical and constitutional element in Luther's depression, but there is no clear evidence that he was ever manic. In modern terms he might be diagnosed as 'a cyclothymic personality, with many mood swings, which, though significant, were never such as to cause a psychosis'.[67]

Another mental condition from which Luther is said to have suffered was an obsessive-compulsive personality disorder. There is certainly evidence that he was obsessive, particularly during his years in the monastery at Erfurt. He was a perfectionist in religion, concerned to rid himself of sin and guilt and to this end he was scrupulous in his religious observance. Such behaviour, however, does not amount to mental illness or disorder.

Luther experienced periods of great anxiety and even of fear, which is not at all surprising when we realise that he lived for many years under the ban of Church and Empire as both a heretic and a rebel. As a result of this ban, his life was frequently in danger for men were commanded to apprehend him and deliver him to the authorities. These periods did not however develop into a chronic anxiety state or neurosis. In the same way although he was the subject of intense persecution by the authorities of both Church and State, we cannot say that he suffered from a state of paranoia.

In summary, we may say that although on occasions Luther did display mental symptoms, these never became permanent features of his personality and never developed into mental illness or disorder.

Also, it is unrealistic to attempt to explain his person, his life and activity on the presumed presence of any mental disorder in his personality. No mental disorder could have produced the historical movement which we call the Reformation.

The only adequate explanation of his life and work is a theological and spiritual one, based on an understanding of the significance of 'the Tower experience' to which we have already referred. This experience changed his whole life, and his work and influence can only be understood in the light of it. It made the existence of evil and its personification in the Devil intensely real, and conversely made gratitude to God for his gift of salvation from sin through the work of Jesus Christ, the constant motive of Luther's life and ministry.

It is on this basis that we must explain those episodes of spiritual crisis in Luther's life and experience which he described as *anfechtungen*. These were regarded by Luther as trials of his faith in God or assaults on that faith by the Devil. They arose from his sense of majesty and holiness of God and his consciousness of the reality of evil in the world and in his own life. They are not symptoms of mental disorder, but episodes in his spiritual experience and development which can only be understood theologically rather than psychologically or psychiatrically. Nevertheless, Luther himself recognised that there was frequently a connection between his *anfechtungen* and attacks of physical symptoms or illness.[68]

Marital History

In the evening of Tuesday 13 June 1525, Luther married Katharine von Bora at Wittenberg. Both Katharine's parents had died when she was young. Her father was an impoverished Roman Catholic nobleman, Hans von Bora. Her mother was Anna von Haubwitz from Bitterfield near Meissen. Katharine had been educated in a convent and when she was sixteen years old she had taken her vows as a nun of the Cistercian Order in the convent at Nimbschen near Leipzig. After eight years as a nun, she had renounced her vows and during the night of 4 April 1523 she and eight other nuns escaped from the convent and were driven on a wagon to Wittenberg, hidden in empty herring barrels. Once they arrived in Wittenberg, Luther arranged for their accommodation. Katharine was lodged with Lucas Cranach the elder, the court painter and the town apothecary, who had just moved into a large new house in the town's market place. However, once settled there she had to wait over two years before Luther proposed to her.

They were married in the monastery at Wittenberg where Luther lived and the ceremony was performed by John Bugenhagen, the parish priest of the Town Church. Lucas Cranach the elder and his wife Barbara acted as sponsors. Including them, only five of his intimate friends were present; not even Melanchthon was there, for Luther had not told him of his intention to get married, anticipating his displeasure. However, two weeks later, on 27 June Luther's parents and fifteen relatives and friends were invited to the postponed wedding feast in Katharine's new home.

Although, at the time of their marriage she was twenty-six years old and Luther was forty-two, the marriage was a very happy one for the couple were very attached to each other.[69] Katharine was a woman of enormous energy and from her habit of early rising, her husband called her 'the morning star of Wittenberg'.[70] On 7 June 1526 she was delivered of their firstborn child, a son who was named Johannes (Hans). Luther reported to his relatives that the boy was healthy and without birth defects, and was 'a good eater and drinker (*homo vorax ac bibax*)'.[71] Altogether they had six children, three boys and three girls. Two of the girls died young, Elizabeth at eight months and Magdalena at thirteen years. Hans became a lawyer and served in the state legal department at Weimar. Martin studied theology but owing to his poor health, he never entered the ministry. The youngest son, Paul (1533-1593), was the most gifted and studied medicine, eventually becoming physician first to the Elector Joachim II of Brandenburg and then to Elector Augustus of Saxony. While only Paul may have attained eminence, none of the Luther children in any way disgraced the good name they bore.[72]

In general, Katie (as her husband called her) seems to have enjoyed good health. The only serious illness recorded of her was in January 1540 following a miscarriage. She was prostrate for weeks and only slowly regained her strength.[73]

She needed all her strength because she had a large house to manage, for Luther had continued to live in the former Augustinian monastery at Wittenberg after all but one of his fellow monks had left. With the departure of the monks the cloister had reverted to the possession of the Elector Frederick the Wise who died five weeks before Luther's wedding. After their wedding, the new Elector John Frederick presented it to Luther and his wife as their home. Soon they had not only a large house, but also a large household of family, students, friends and servants, to say nothing of their domestic animals, which Katie proved herself able to manage very efficiently.

Luther Needs a Doctor

The only injury of which we have any knowledge was sustained by Luther when he was a student at Erfurt. He was travelling home to Mansfeld at Easter 1503 with a friend and when he broke into a run soon after leaving Erfurt, his short student's sword accidentally pierced his left leg and cut open an artery which bled profusely. His companion left him in the care of some villagers and ran the half-mile back to Erfurt to call a surgeon. However, the surgeon found the wound difficult to close and so Luther was carried back to Erfurt. During the night while he was in bed, the wound broke down and he almost died from the loss of blood.[74] It was during his convalescence from this injury that he taught himself to play the lute, an accomplishment which became a frequent means of relaxation in later times.[75]

So far as we know, this may have been the first time that Luther had needed the attention of a doctor. As we shall see, he frequently needed medical attention in later life and he was not uncritical of his doctors and the treatment they gave him. He accepted that the physician is God's mender of the body as the theologian is the mender of the soul.[76] Nevertheless when he recalled his illness in Schmalkalden (to which we shall refer on a later page) during which he was much worked on by his physicians, he described that man as wretched who relies on the help of physicians. However, he felt at that time he had to obey his physicians or they would think that he did not take care of his body.[77]

On another occasion after he been prescribed a rigid diet he said that to live medically was to live wretchedly and he would eat what he liked and die when God willed.[78] Nevertheless, once when he was asked by the burgomaster of Wittenberg whether it was permissible to make use of medicine, he replied, 'Do you eat when you are hungry? If you do, you may also use medicine, which is God's creation as truly as food or drink and whatever else we need for sustaining life'.[79]

However, for the first forty years of his life Luther enjoyed surprisingly good health and we have few references to any illnesses he suffered during these years. It was only as he became a public figure after he nailed his ninety-five theses concerning the practice of granting Indulgences by the Pope, to the oaken doors of the Castle Church of All Saints at Wittenberg about noon on 31 October 1517, that he began to have significant episodes of ill-health. These were initially related to periods of external stress such as his journeys to Augsburg (1518) and Worms (1521).[80] It was early in January 1527 when he was forty-three years old that he began to experience the cardiac symptoms which were to recur on several occasions and which were to be associated with his death.

Fevers and Infections

The earliest reference to an illness dates from his schooldays at Magdeburg when Luther (then aged 14) fell ill with a fever. He became very thirsty and was refused anything to drink by his physician. However, when the people with whom he was lodging had gone off to Church and left him alone, he crawled to the kitchen and drank the contents of a large jug of water. When he returned to his bed he fell into a deep sleep from which he awoke to find his fever gone. In view of his later history of heart disease it has been suggested that this illness was rheumatic fever, but this seems to be very unlikely.[81]

There are several references in Luther's letters and his *Table Talk* to his not feeling well and sometimes it is mentioned that he has a fever. The nature of these attacks of fever is not mentioned. On one occasion he mentions that his friend Melanchthon has fallen ill with a 'tertian fever'.[82] This may have been malaria, but he never describes his own fevers in this way, nor does he use the term 'ague'.[83]

On one occasion in 1523 he mentions that he 'caught a fever from a bath (*febris e balneo contraxi*)'. Unfortunately this detail does not help us to identify the fever. However, this particular febrile illness is important historically because an ambiguous medical report was written about it which gave rise to the completely unfounded rumour that Luther was suffering from syphilis.[84]

From time to time we read of Luther suffering from an upper respiratory infection and episodes of coughing, even occasionally of his losing his voice and being unable to lecture to his students. An example of this occurred during an influenza epidemic in April 1529 when he developed a racking cough and lost his voice, remaining hoarse and unable to preach or lecture until the beginning of May.[85] On one occasion in March 1541 he suffered an upper respiratory infection which was complicated by an acute infection of the left middle ear. This caused him severe giddiness, tinnitus, deafness and acute pain which was only relieved when the ear drum ruptured and a discharge appeared which became purulent and foul-smelling (*immundus fluxu auris*) and persisted until the beginning of May when his hearing returned to normal but the tinnitus continued.[86]

In a letter dated 31 July 1529, Luther tells of the appearance of an epidemic of the Sweating Sickness which was then sweeping Germany and had reached Wittenberg.[87] Because this disease first appeared in England in 1485 it was commonly called the English Sweat (*Sudor Anglicus*).[88] On 26 August, Luther wakened up bathed in sweat and with the other symptoms of this disease. However, he did not believe that this condition was a physical disease but was hysterical in origin, and so he got up and shrugged it off as he had advised his colleagues to do when he had driven them from their beds.[89]

Another epidemic disease which from time to time made its appearance at Wittenberg was bubonic plague. There was an outbreak in October 1516, but the most serious outbreak was in 1527 with the result that in August of that year, the university staff and students moved ninety miles south to Jena to escape the infection. Luther and three of his ministerial colleagues, however, felt it was their duty to remain in Wittenberg. Although his own house was transformed into a hospital, he and his family escaped the infection and all those who had been admitted to Luther's house recovered. Only Katie's pigs were lost! However, several of their Wittenberg friends died in this epidemic.[90] The university staff and students did not return to Wittenberg until January 1536.[91] In response to requests from John Hess, the Lutheran pastor at Breslau, for advice on a question which was of universal interest at this time, Luther wrote a pamphlet entitled *Whether One may Flee from a Deadly Plague*. He felt that people might justifiably do so, but those with official, professional or pastoral responsibilities should not do so.[92]

Also from time to time Luther appears to have had infective gastro-intestinal conditions which might have been accompanied by fever, but fever is not mentioned. In October 1518, during the final day of his journey on foot to appear before the Dominican Cardinal Cajetan in Augsburg, he developed an intestinal infection and became very weak and had to hire a wagon for the last three miles, but again there is no mention of fever on this occasion.[93] Once in August 1535 when he was at home he had an acute attack of what was probably bacillary dysentery and passed fifteen stools in two days.[94] On Sunday 9 July 1538 he was unable to preach because he had diarrhoea and when his physician saw him next day he gave him an enema and prescribed coriander seeds (*Coriandrum sativum*). This reminded Luther of the story of the man who had also been prescribed coriander, and thought that his physician had said 'calendars'. According to Luther the patient duly bought four calendars, cut them up and swallowed the fragments in four doses.[95]

'A Cathedral Chapter'

On one occasion he said that his head was like 'a cathedral chapter', the noisy routine business meeting of the staff of a cathedral.[96] This was his description of what his constant headaches, tinnitus, dizziness and giddiness felt like. We have already mentioned one acute cause of these symptoms when he developed a middle ear infection in March 1541, but he suffered from them chronically and for some years before he contracted this infection. The combination of these symptoms might suggest that he suffered from Ménière's syndrome, although headache is not described as part of this syndrome and also in Luther's case there is no mention of the progressive deafness which usually does form part of it. A sufficient cause for these symptoms can be found in the situation of stress, anxiety and overwork in which he lived constantly.

His headaches could be very severe and interfere with his study and writing. Occasionally he describes them as 'throbbing' as if they may have been vascular in origin, although his description does not suggest they were migrainous in nature.[97] The tinnitus appears to have first affected him in his left ear in July 1527, but it appeared periodically after this and troubled him greatly. When it affected him he often could not work and had to give up reading or writing and lie down.[98]

Whether refractive errors caused any of Luther's headaches we do not know, but we do know that he needed to wear spectacles from at least 1525. In February of that year his colleague Wenceslaus Link sent him a pair from Nuremberg.[99] In a letter to his wife written in July 1530 from Fortress (*Veste*) Coburg where he was staying to be on hand for the Diet of Augsburg, he complains about an unsatisfactory pair of spectacles made for him by Christian Düring, the Wittenberg goldsmith.[100] Later, his sight began to deteriorate especially in his left eye, so that in a letter of January 1546 he says he is now 'one-eyed (*monoculus*)'.[101]

'Junker Georg'

Luther's courageous stand at the Diet of Worms in April 1521 meant that his life was now more in danger than ever before. Although he had come to Worms under a safe-conduct provided by the emperor, this could be revoked at any time as one had been revoked in the case of Jan Hus, the Bohemian Reformer, who had then been burned at the stake in Constance over a century earlier. The result was that Luther, having previously been warned what was to happen,[102] was ambushed and kidnapped on Saturday 4 May by a mounted party of his friends near the castle of Altenstein on his homeward journey through the dense Thuringian forest. After lengthy detours to shake off any possible pursuers, the party arrived at the Wartburg, a large and ancient castle belonging to the Elector Frederick the Wise of Saxony who had assumed the role of Luther's protector. The castle lay within the Elector's own territory and stood almost untenanted on a steep hill about a mile south of Eisenach. Luther spent most of the next year there, so effectively hidden that many regarded him as dead. He grew a beard and assumed the dress and identity of a country squire under the alias of 'Junker Georg (Squire George)', constantly wearing a cap to disguise his tonsure until his hair grew again. He occupied two rooms in the castle, a sitting room and a bedroom, situated above the warden's own quarters and provided with modest furniture. These rooms were reached by a movable stairway or step-ladder which was raised on a chain and locked each night for reasons of security.[103]

When he was kidnapped, Luther had snatched up his Hebrew Bible and his Greek New Testament so that he had something to read in his unaccustomed quiet solitude in the Wartburg. After less than eleven weeks there, he had translated the New Testament into German using the second edition of the Greek text which had been published by Erasmus in Basle in 1519, a feat which gave rise to the saying that Erasmus had laid the egg which Luther hatched. Luther's translation was thoroughly revised by Melanchthon to be published in Wittenberg in a folio edition of three thousand copies on 21 September 1522, and so was referred to as 'The September Testament'. In spite of its large size and costing the same as a large horse, this first edition was soon exhausted and by December a new and corrected edition was ready, which was called 'The December Testament'. This translation was later revised several times and when the translation of the Old Testament was added to it in 1534, it became for the Modern High German language and German literature what the Authorised Version of the Bible almost a century later became for the Elizabethan language and English literature.

In addition to his work on this translation, Luther's pen was busy writing model Sunday sermons and homilies (or postils) for the use of Lutheran pastors and the congregation at Wittenberg, great numbers of letters to his friends and colleagues, and numerous pamphlets and treatises on a variety of subjects. One of these treatises was *On Monastic Vows* which he dedicated to his father. In this elaborate treatise, dated 21 November 1521, Luther maintained that the current monastic vows could not be justified from Scripture and therefore were not binding. It was this view which led to his final discarding of his black Augustinian cowl on 16 October 1524 after almost twenty years as a monk,[104] and then to his marriage to the former nun Katharine von Bora in June of the following year, to which I have already referred.

'My Vexatious Handicap'

Luther's stand at the Diet of Worms in April 1521 was a watershed in the history of Europe and in many aspects of his own life too. His confinement in the Wartburg meant a change in his life style, which had at least one important medical result. He began to suffer from severe constipation. His regular and ample meals began to fill out his gaunt physical frame, but were more than his digestive system could cope with, after the simple fare he had been accustomed to as a monk. His enforced lack of exercise, apart from a walk in the castle grounds or a ride in the woods, did nothing to aid his digestion either. To begin with, Luther dismissed his constipation as 'a little ailment' but it got worse and in a letter to Melanchthon he admits that it has become a 'vexatious handicap (*molestia vexatus*)'.[105]

In order to keep in touch with his friends outside, Luther wrote regular monthly letters to them, and all the letters written between May and October 1521 contain vivid references to 'my constipation' and its results.[106] On 12 May he writes to Melanchthon:

> The elimination is so hard that I am forced to press with all my strength, even to the point of perspiration, and the longer I delay the worse it gets.[107]

In July he obtains purgative medicine from his friend Spalatin and finds elimination easier.[108] Nevertheless, he still has a stool only every fourth or fifth day even with medicine.[109] The constipation had other effects too. It produced an anal fissure which caused him pain and soreness, and was kept open by the continued passage of hard stools. The straining also produced internal haemorrhoids which prolapsed as a fleshy mass when his bowels opened.[110] However, by October he can write to Spalatin and say:

> At last my behind and my bowels have reconciled themselves to me. Therefore I need no further medicine and am completely healthy as before.[111]

Luther, of course, suffered from constipation at other times too but no later experience was quite so severe as that which he had during his stay in the Wartburg.

'My Torturer the Stone'

It was in March 1526, when he was forty-two years old, that Luther first mentioned that he was having attacks of renal colic and it was not until the following June that he reported some relief from them.[112]

More attacks occurred in 1536. They began in April of that year and were so severe that he wanted to die rather than endure them. At the beginning of June he passed several small stones with a great deal of pain. This appears to be the first time that he had actually passed stones.[113]

However, worse was to come. On 7 February 1537, Luther arrived in Schmalkalden, a small town in Hesse, to attend a meeting of the Protestant princes and theologians. The town was full to capacity and his lodgings were not satisfactory, in particular he complained of having to sleep in wet sheets.[114] The day after he arrived he passed a small stone and some blood *per urethram* with very little pain, but on the 11th and 18th he had severe pain although he passed no stones. On Sunday the 18th, the personal physician of his host, the Landgrave of Hesse, gave him an enema which produced a persistent diarrhoea but did not relieve his pain and only increased his weakness. On the 19th he was unable to pass urine and this retention of urine lasted for eight days.[115]

There was no dearth of physicians in Schmalkalden for each of the eight princes attending the meeting there, was accompanied by his own personal physician. In addition, on 20 February, Luther asked that his friend Dr Georg Sturtz of Erfurt should be sent for too, and he came bringing medicines which were not available in the little town, because it had no apothecary. Then on the 24th, a lithotomist (*Steinschneider*) was called in from Waltershausen to be on hand to operate if required. However, they all failed to relieve his pain and his urinary retention, but it was not for want of trying.

Once the urinary retention occurred, several methods of treatment were tried. First, the physicians increased Luther's fluid intake. He said afterwards that they gave him as much to drink as if he had been 'a big ox'.[116] Then they prepared a broth made from almonds which he drank. They applied hot compresses to his abdomen to soothe the pain. They massaged his perineum and urethra until he complained that these felt numb and lifeless. Eventually the surgeons considered cutting him for stone in order to remove the cause of the obstruction, but they decided against it. The Elector's surgeon had a gold bougie made, but even this was not able to dislodge the obstructing stone when inserted into the urethra. His wife Katie contributed to his treatment by sending him a medicine made of ground cloves of garlic boiled with fresh horse droppings (*allium et stercus equinum*) prepared according to a prescription from the *Dreckapotheke* (Faecal pharmacopoeia).[117] Later, Luther told her that the medicine was disgusting to swallow and had been of no help.[118]

After a week of intense suffering, the early signs of acute renal failure or uraemia appeared as Luther became euphoric and began to vomit.[119] On the 25th he insisted on being taken back to Wittenberg, saying that if he was going to die (as he thought he was) he preferred to die at home. He set off the next day in the Elector's private carriage accompanied by Dr Sturtz and several colleagues. Two men walked beside the carriage in order to try to minimise the jolting caused by the rough roads, which caused Luther such excruciating pain. After travelling for about ten miles they stopped at an inn at Tambach. Here the jolting of the journey accomplished what the doctors had failed to accomplish, for during the night he began to pass urine. As he put it in a letter to Melanchthon, written early on the morning of the 27th, his 'silver stream' had been restored. He told his wife that once he was able to pass urine again, he had passed about one *Stübig* or three to four litres in the space of two hours.[120]

Next day they arrived at Gotha where Luther had another severe attack of pain with the result that on March 1st he passed six stones, one as large as a hazelnut. Although the crisis was past, Luther still believed that he was going to die, and at Gotha, after making his confession to John Bugenhagen, the Wittenberg pastor who was accompanying him, he dictated a farewell document to his family and friends and commended his soul to God.[121] The next morning he expressed some surprise when he woke up, saying 'I lay down last night expecting to be a corpse today'.[122] However, after this he began to improve and over the next two weeks, Luther and his friends continued their slow journey in short stages until they finally arrived in Wittenberg on 14 March. It was not a pleasant journey as he had another two days of anuria and continued to pass more small stones until he arrived home suffering from weakness, abdominal pain, vomiting and insomnia. It was not until July that he had recovered enough strength to resume his preaching and lecturing. In November he was still passing stones and at the end of the year he still had to cut his sermons short because of weakness. It was at this time that Augustine Schurf, one of his physicians, predicted that he would die of a stroke. However, Luther was not impressed by this; only a blessed death interested him.[123]

Although there are references in Luther's letters to attacks of stone in the years 1538, 1539, 1543 and 1545, he never again experienced so severe and prolonged an attack as he did at Schmalkalden in 1537, in which his life was really in danger. They did, however, often prevent him from riding a horse because of the pain that this caused. The last attacks of pain appear to have been in the summer of 1545. One occurred on 2 August during his consecration of the new Lutheran bishop of Merseberg and he had to be supported as he left the cathedral in pain.[124] These attacks were so severe that he said he would prefer 'death to such a tyrant'. It was at this time that he spoke in a letter to Amsdorf of 'my torturer the stone (*carnifex meus calculus*)'.[125] In February 1546 he writes to his wife from Eisleben to say that the stone no longer bothers him.[126]

The cause of the renal stones from which Luther suffered, appears to have been gout which on one occasion he observed was an English disease, while the stone was peculiar to Germany.[127] Clinical experience has not upheld the truth of this observation, but there is no doubt that urinary calculi were very common in Germany and in Europe generally in the Middle Ages and later. Luther showed other classical features of gout with attacks of acute pain in the small joints of the feet which are specifically mentioned in the years 1533 and 1538.[128] In 1538 he began to use a walking stick because of the pain caused by the gout.[129] The plaster casts of his hands made after his death show the typical deformities of a gouty arthritis.[130] On one occasion Luther attributed his gout and his stone to the drinking of bad wine.[131]

Apart from gout, Luther appears to have suffered from other forms of arthritis too. For instance, he writes to Martin Bucer in Strasburg in 1536 and mentions that he has had 'unbearably excruciating pains' in his left hip which have kept him in bed for two weeks.[132]

The End Draws Near

As the year 1545 neared its close, it was clear to Luther and his friends from his physical weakness and weariness, that he would not live much longer.

He had begun to lecture on the book of Genesis on 1 June 1535 and on 17 November 1545 he drew this long course of lectures to an end with the following words to his students:

> This is now the book of Genesis. God grant that after me others will do better. I can do no more. I am weak. Pray God for me that he may grant me a good and blessed last hour.[133]

He celebrated his sixty-second birthday with his friends in Wittenberg on 10 January 1546, and a week later he preached his last sermon in the Castle Church there.[134]

Finally, on 23 January in bitterly cold weather, Luther set out from Wittenberg to Eisleben (a distance of some eighty miles) on what was to prove to be his last journey. He had been called upon to mediate in a dispute between Albrecht and Gebhard, the two Counts of Mansfeld, who were brothers but had fallen out over Albrecht's new demands for greater control of the copper-smelters and increased revenue from the smeltermasters, one of whom was Luther's own brother James.[135] He had already paid two visits to Eisleben in this connection but had not succeeded in settling the dispute, and now was called upon for a third time. Although he was now in his sixty-third year and very weary and worn, nevertheless he felt it was his duty to go, as Mansfeld was where he had been brought up. His friend Melanchthon had accompanied him on the two previous visits, but this time he was unable to go with him as he too was suffering from the stone and constipation. However, Luther did not want for company on this journey, as he took with him his three sons so that they could visit the place where their father had been born and baptised.

After being held up at Halle for three days by the swollen River Saale which was full of floodwater and great blocks of ice, they reached the outskirts of Eisleben on 28 January, when Luther felt unwell. In a letter to Melanchthon dated 1 February, he describes how he fainted in the extreme cold as he walked on his journey and had an attack of what he said Melanchthon would call 'palpitations (*humor ventriculi*)'. He perspired, became short of breath, felt coldness and stiffness of his left arm and tightness around the heart. He was taken to a nearby house where hot towels were applied to his chest. However, his symptoms gradually passed off and he completed his journey in a carriage.[136] When he arrived in Eisleben he was accommodated in the official residence of John Albrecht, the town clerk, next to St Andrew's Church in the south-eastern part of the town. Two rooms were set apart for his use on the first floor, one as a sitting-room and the other as a bedroom. Although the house is described as elegant, some parts do not appear to have been in good repair because Luther complained to his wife of plaster falling off the wall of his 'secret chamber' (the privy) over two days. When workmen were brought in to repair the wall, they dislodged a large stone from the wallhead which narrowly missed falling on Luther's head and squashing him like a mouse in a mouse trap, as he described it to his wife.[137]

'Myself in a Coffin'

By 16 February the dispute had been settled and according to the record of his *Table Talk* for that day, Luther said,

> I will now no longer tarry, but set myself to go to Wittenberg and there lay myself in a coffin and give the worms a fat doctor to feed upon.[138]

But this was not to be. The next day he did not feel well and kept to his rooms. Before supper he complained of pain and tightness of his chest and was massaged with hot towels to improve his circulation. But he insisted on coming down to supper and eating a hearty meal with his companions, during which the conversation turned on the topics of death and the world to come.[139] After supper he went upstairs to his sitting-room where he began his customary evening prayer at the open window, after which the pain and tightness in his chest returned and forced him to lie down on the leather sofa, where he was again treated with massage and hot towels. One of his colleagues obtained a concoction of grated unicorn horn from Count Albrecht and gave it to him, after which he went to sleep.[140] He slept for about two or more hours when he awoke about ten o'clock and asked for his bed to be warmed. When this was done, he walked through to his bedroom and lay down on his bed and slept again. About one o'clock in the morning, he was wakened by another attack of pain and got up and returned to the sitting-room to lie on the sofa there again, where his companions sought to treat him for the third time with hot towels and massage to his chest.

They then summoned their hosts, the town clerk and his wife, who in turn called in the two town physicians and finally Count Albrecht and his wife Anna, who was familiar with medicines. The pain and anguish continued and when he began to feel cold and to perspire, Luther realised he was dying and recited the words of the text John 3:16 three times and then said, 'I am going, and shall render up my spirit'. He then commended his soul to God three times in the words of Psalm 31:5: 'Into thine hand I commit my spirit: thou hast redeemed me, O Lord God of Truth'. Countess Anna tried to revive him by rubbing him with rose vinegar and *aqua vitae* but to no avail.[141]

In a final word he confirmed to the assembled company that he died trusting in the Lord Jesus Christ and in the doctrine he had himself taught. He then turned on to his right side and fell asleep again. Fifteen minutes later, at about a quarter-to-three in the morning of Thursday, 18 February 1546, Doctor Martin Luther took a deep breath and gave up his spirit.[142] Just after he had died, the physicians summoned John Landau, the town apothecary, to administer an enema in an attempt to revive him, but this attempt was unsuccessful.[143]

Although Luther had died at Eisleben where he had been born, the Elector John Frederick insisted that he should be buried at Wittenberg. Consequently, his body was placed in a pewter coffin and after first lying in state in St Andrew's Church where he had preached his last four sermons, it was taken to Wittenberg. On 22 February the body was buried in the Castle Church there in a grave which had been prepared beneath the floor of the Church and directly in front of the pulpit from which he had preached so often.[144] The funeral sermon was preached by John Bugenhagen, the parish priest of Wittenberg, and the eulogy was delivered by Luther's friend and colleague of many years, Philip Melanchthon, who represented the University.[145]

Apoplexy or Heart Attack?

The two physicians who examined Luther's body on the day after his death disagreed about the cause of his death. One diagnosed apoplexy because he thought that one side of his mouth was drawn down and the whole of the right side of his body was discoloured (*visa enim est tortura oris et exterum latus totum infuscatum*).[146] The other physician thought he had died from heart disease as he could not conceive that so holy a man as Luther could have been struck down by the hand of God, i.e., that he could have had 'a stroke' which is the literal meaning of apoplexy. Melanchthon accepted the diagnosis of heart disease and most of the standard biographies of Luther have followed him.[147]

We have, of course, no detailed clinical description of the physical signs which Luther might have shown during the two days or so before he died. However, if he had suffered from an apoplectic attack we would have expected him to lose consciousness, to show signs of muscular weakness or paralysis and perhaps to have difficulty in speaking if he had remained conscious. None of these features appear to have been present in Luther's case. He did not lapse into unconsciousness until a short time before he died. He showed no signs of hemiplegia or muscular paralysis and was able to walk between his bedroom and his sitting room without any difficulty until less than two hours before his death. He was able to change his position in bed, and fifteen minutes before he died he turned over on to his right side and fell asleep. He had no difficulty in speaking, for in his last hours he recited passages of Scripture and commended his soul to God in the hearing of his friends. A few minutes before he died he was able to assure them that he died trusting in Christ and in the doctrine which he had preached. We conclude, therefore, that it seems unlikely that apoplexy was the cause of Luther's death.

What has often been lost sight of in the consideration of the cause of Luther's death is that he had a long history of cardiac symptoms similar to those which occurred in the twenty-four hours or so before he died.

As we have already mentioned, their first appearance was early in January 1527 when he was seized with pain and a tightness in his chest. He said that it felt like a sudden clotting of the blood around the precordial area. He was able to treat this attack with a folk remedy which consisted of the watery extract of the blessed thistle (*Aqua cardui benedicti*) and this alleviated the pain. Afterwards, Luther wrote with some pride to tell his friend Spalatin he had done this, although he said that 'the doctors neglect and even have no knowledge of the power of this remedy (*quamquam medici neglecta vel ignota potius*)'.[148] Then in July of the same year he had a severe fainting spell and was treated with hot compresses to his chest, and although he was said to become very cold and thought he was going to die, there is no mention of any specifically local cardiac symptoms on this occasion.[149]

He had another attack of 'extraordinary faintness in his heart' at 4am on 22 January 1532 accompanied by a ringing in his ears. After inspecting his urine, the physician said that he had been close to apoplexy, but would recover from this attack of illness.[150]

During the year 1535, Luther had several episodes of illness including upper respiratory infections and diarrhoea which interfered with his teaching and preaching. On December 19th of the following year he appears to have suffered a heart attack which was so severe that it was feared that he was going to die, but he recovered although he was left very weak.[151]   During his attack of bacillary dysentery in July 1538 which lasted for over a week, Luther mentions in his *Table Talk* that he had an irregular pulse (*pulsus variationem*). No details of the character of the irregularity are given, although Luther does say that he was reassured by his physician that it was not serious.[152]

There would appear also to be no doubt that Luther suffered a heart attack in the severe wintry weather of 28 January 1546 as he completed his last journey to Eisleben, which we have already described. This attack may have been brought on by the intense cold encountered on that journey.

His final attack of chest pain came on February 17th and in the early morning of the following day he died. In view of his clinical history, it seems not inappropriate to suggest that the cause of Luther's death was a heart attack or myocardial infarction and not apoplexy.

Did Luther Have High Blood Pressure?

Whichever diagnosis we accept of the cause of Luther's death it means that the underlying cause was cardiovascular in nature. Since a common cause of both apoplexy and heart attacks, at least in modern experience, is high blood pressure or hypertension, it seems appropriate to consider the question of whether Luther suffered from high blood pressure.

There are a number of factors which were present in Luther's case which modern cardiologists associate with the occurrence of high blood pressure. These are age, stress, obesity and a high salt intake. Luther was in his mid-forties when he began to experience cardiac symptoms, which is not old by modern standards, but in his time people began to age earlier than they do today. There is no doubt about the mental and spiritual stress under which Luther lived and we referred to this above when we considered factors which affected his health. There is no doubt either about the increasing obesity which he displayed in his later years.

A fourth factor may well have been the high salt content of his diet. Luther has been described as frequently eating nothing during the day but bread and salt. On one occasion when he was writing his commentary on the Psalms, Luther shut himself away for three days and three nights with nothing to eat but bread and salt. His wife became so concerned about him that she called a locksmith to open the door of his room, when they found him well but lost in deep meditation. His favourite dish was said to be pea-soup and herring and this would add more salt to his diet because the herring were pickled in brine for their preservation.[153]

Finally, there is a fifth factor in Luther's medical history which is probably of more specific significance for the causation of his high blood pressure than these four more general factors. For years he had suffered from kidney stones which from time to time produced attacks of renal colic and urinary obstruction. Even when they were not producing these symptoms, the formation and presence of these stones would lead to damage to the structure and function of one or both kidneys. This in turn would affect the normal mechanism for the control of blood pressure in the body, which is dependent on the kidney. The result would be the appearance of raised blood pressure secondary to the disease of the kidney, a condition which is usually described as *renal hypertension*.[154]

'The Little Fountain'

One of the recognised methods of lowering blood pressure is by reducing the volume of circulating blood. The long-established practice for doing this was by the removal of blood from the circulation by blood-letting or phlebotomy, a procedure which usually consisted of the slitting open with a knife of one of the veins of the front of the forearm after applying a bandage or tourniquet to the arm. The blood was then caught in a bowl as it flowed out. In earlier times this was practised on a quite empirical basis because the physiology and pathology of blood pressure were not understood. All that was known was that some patients benefited by having some amount of their blood taken off from their veins. Many of these may have suffered from high blood pressure.

The only mention of actual phlebotomy performed on Luther was after he fell ill at Eisenach on his way to the Diet of Worms in April 1521.[155] No details are available of the nature of this illness, but it appears to have been very severe and left him very weak for he writes to Spalatin from Frankfurt-on-Main that he continued to be very ill 'in a way which has previously been unknown to me'. Nevertheless, in spite of his weak condition he was determined to reach Worms, and he did.[156]

There are, however, references to blood-letting by means of a *fontanella*. Meaning literally 'a little fountain', this term refers to an ulcer occurring naturally or a wound artificially produced by incision, cautery or the application of some caustic substance to the skin. This wound or ulcer was artificially kept open to permit chronic blood-letting by oozing. This was believed to counteract faintness and dizziness.

Luther was first reported to have an ulcer of his left calf in January 1525.[157] This appears to have become chronic as it was mentioned in several subsequent years. It was most probably a chronic venous ulcer resulting from the presence of varicose veins or a thrombophlebitis of the deep veins of Luther's left lower limb.[158] From at least the summer of 1534, a *fontanella* from this ulcer was maintained on the recommendation of Dr Matthaeus Ratzeberger, the personal physician of the Elector.[159] It was kept open artificially by the periodic application of a stone of caustic material (*lapillus corrosivus*) which was probably bluestone composed of crude copper sulphate.[160]

Dorothy, the Countess of Mansfeld did not agree with Dr Ratzeberger's recommendation and sent Luther a long letter of advice. In her view, Luther should allow the *fontanella* to heal. He should take more exercise and use sneezing powder. His fainting attacks should be treated with white aquavit and his cardiac and digestive symptoms with yellow aquavit.[161]

However, Luther preferred to keep his *fontanella* open and so he was dismayed to find that it had almost healed when he arrived in Eisleben from Wittenberg in January 1546. The result was that he wrote to Melanchthon in Wittenberg to ask him to send a messenger to Eisleben with a caustic stone in order that he might keep the wound open.[162] After Luther's death, Dr Ratzeberger expressed the opinion that the healing of the *fontanella* could very well have contributed to his death. There were of course no means of measuring human blood pressure in Luther's day and so we cannot answer the question at the head of this section with any certainty.

It does not seem unreasonable, however, to believe that Luther did suffer from high blood pressure which was secondary to disease of his kidneys, the result of the formation and presence of kidney stones, and that his death was due to one of the recognised complications of high blood pressure, namely, myocardial infarction.[163]

NOTES AND REFERENCES
FOR CHAPTER 1

Key to abbreviations

CR = *Corpus Reformatorum, Philippi Melanchthon Opera*; C.G.Bretschneider & H.E.Bindseil (eds) (Halle: C.A.Schwetschke, 1834-1860), 28 vols.

LW = *Luther's Works* (American edition) J.Pelikan & H.T.Lehmann (eds) (Philadelphia: Fortress Press, 1955-1986), 55 vols.

WA = *D.Martin Luthers Werke: Kritische Gesamtausgabe* (Weimar: Hermann Böhlhaus Nachfolger 1883-1983), 60 vols.

WA Br = *D.Martin Luthers Werke: Kritische Gesamtausgabe. Briefwechsel* (Weimar: Hermann Böhlaus Nachfolger 1930-1978), 15 vols. These volumes contain 4,335 letters written by or to Luther.

WA TR = *D.Martin Luthers Werke: Kritische Gesamtausgabe. Tischreden* (Weimar: Hermann Böhlaus Nachfolger, 1912-1921), 6 vols. These volumes contain 7,075 of Luther's comments made to his guests at meals, normally referred to in English as 'Table Talk'. These comments have each been given a serial reference number by the editors.

Key to authors and sources quoted

Atkinson = J.Atkinson, *Martin Luther & the Birth of Protestantism* (Harmondsworth: Penguin Books, 1968).

Bainton = R.Bainton, *Here I Stand: A life of Martin Luther* (London: Hodder & Stoughton, 1951).

Boehmer = H.Boehmer, *Road to Reformation: Martin Luther to the Year 1521* (Philadelphia: Mühlenberg Press, 1946).

Bornkamm = H.Bornkamm, *Luther in Mid-career (1521-1530)* (Philadelphia: Fortress Press, 1983).

Brecht = M.Brecht, *Martin Luther.* English Translation by J.L.Schaaf (Minneapolis: Fortress Press, 1985-1993), 3 vols.

Brendler = G.Brendler, *Martin Luther: Theology and Revolution* (New York: Oxford University Press, 1991).

Davies = G.Davies, *Genius and Grace: Sketches from a Psychiatrist's Notebook* (London: Hodder & Stoughton, 1992), 23-49: 'Martin Luther'.

Erikson = E.H.Erikson, *Young Man Luther: A Study in Psychoanalysis and History* (London: Faber & Faber, 1959).

Freytag = G.Freytag, *Martin Luther* (Chicago & London: Open Court Publishing Co., 1897).

Grisar = H.Grisar, *Luther* (London: Kegan Paul, Trench, Trübner & Co., 1917), 6 vols.

Haile = H.G.Haile, *Luther: An Experiment in Biography* (Princeton, New Jersey: Princeton University Press, 1980).

Jacobs = H.E.Jacobs, *Martin Luther: The Hero of the Reformation* (New York: G.P.Putnam's Sons, 1898).

Johnson = R.A.Johnson (ed) *Psychohistory and Religion: The Case of the Young Man Luther* (Philadelphia: Fortress Press, 1977).

Köstlin = J.Köstlin, *Life of Luther: Translated from the German* (London: Longmans, Green & Co., 1905).

Kuiper = B.K.Kuiper, *Martin Luther: The Formative Years* (Grand Rapids, Michigan: Eerdmans Publishing Co., 1933).

Manns = P.Manns, *Martin Luther: An Illustrated Biography* (New York: Crossroad Publishing Co., 1983).

Mackinnon = J.Mackinnon, *Luther and the Reformation* (London: Longmans, Green & Co., 1925-1930), 4 vols.

Marius = R.Marius, *Martin Luther: The Christian between Life and Death* (Cambridge, Massachusetts: Harvard University Press, 1999).

Michelet = M.Michelet, *The Life of Luther written by Himself* (London: George Bell & Sons, 1882).

Oberman = H.A.Oberman, *Luther: Man between God and the Devil* (London: Fontana Press 1993).

Panel = E.Bacchus & H.K.Scatliff (eds), 'Martin Luther: A Panel Postmortem' in *Chicago Medicine* (1966) **69**:108-116.

Rupp = E.G.Rupp, *Encyclopaedia Britannica* (Chicago: University of Chicago Press, 1988), **23**:364-372, art. 'Luther'.

Rupp & Drewery = E.G.Rupp & Drewery B (eds), *Martin Luther* (London: Edward Arnold, 1970).

Sears = G.Sears, *Luther: His Mental and Spiritual History* (London: Religious Tract Society, 1850).

Siggins = I.D.K.Siggins (ed), *Luther* (Edinburgh: Oliver & Boyd, 1972).

Smith = P.Smith, *The Life and Letters of Martin Luther* (Boston and New York: Houghton Mifflin Co., 1911).

Schwiebert = E.G.Schwiebert, *Luther and his Times* (St Louis, Missouri: Concordia Publishing House, 1950).

¹   Siggins 1.

²   Schwiebert 100. Cp H.Schmidt (ed), *Martini Lutheri Opera Latina.*
(Frankfurt-on-Main & Erlangen, 1865), **1**:15-24. Extracts from the
autobiography are given in translation in Rupp & Drewery 5 & 173-175.

³   Siggins 31.

⁴   Melanchthon's biography of Luther is to be found in CR **6**: 155-170.
Philip Melanchthon (1497-1560) was the first professor of Greek at Wittenberg
University and a close friend and colleague of Martin Luther with whose
views he was in full sympathy.

⁵   One of these short biographical accounts is by Dr Matthaeus Ratzeberger
(1501-1559), physician to the Counts of Mansfeld, who often attended Luther
medically and was apparently related to him by marriage. However, this
biography is not regarded as altogether reliable for Ratzeberger is believed to
have added numerous embellishments to his account. It was probably he who
invented the story of Luther's throwing an inkpot at the Devil who was
tormenting him in his study at the Wartburg during his stay there in 1521.
Although an ink-stain on the wall behind the stove in the north-east corner of
the room is regularly shown to tourists, the traditional story of its origin is
apocryphal for 'nowhere in Luther's writings, not even in the *Table Talk*, is there
a reference to throwing an inkwell at the devil' (Schwiebert 519). This story first
appeared in 1591 and afterwards the ink stain became a standard feature of each
of the houses occupied by Luther (Bornkamm 13). For example a similar ink-
stain used to be shown in the room at the Castle of Coburg where Luther
stayed in 1530 (Köstlin 213).

⁶   Brecht **1**:3-6; Jacobs 5; Kuiper 16. Luther's relations are said to have filled
half the countryside around Möhra (Freytag 5).

⁷   In the standard modern biographies the maiden names of Luther's
mother and grandmother are commonly given as those of Ziegler and
Lindemann respectively, but it has now been established that Luther's
mother was a Lindemann and his grandmother a Ziegler. See I.D.K.Siggins,
'Luther's mother Margarethe' in *Harvard Theological Review* (1978) **71**: 125-
150, especially the genealogical table on page 140. For a much fuller
consideration see I.D.K.Siggins, *Luther and his Mother* (Philadelphia: Fortress
Press, 1981).

⁸   WA TR **5**:98 no.5362; WA TR **5**:558 no.6250. With the intensive
development of the copper-mining industry there, the Eisleben-Mansfeld
area became an important centre for the study and practice of occupational
medicine. See W.Kaiser, 'Eisleben and the Mansfeld area in medical history'
in *Z Gesamte Inn Med* (1983) **38**(20):539-546 (Oct 15).

⁹   It is possible that Martin Luther had an older brother who had already
died before Martin was born, but Luther's reference to this possibility in WA
TR **5**:95 no.5362 is unclear. Cp Brecht **1**:2. The house in which Luther was
born was burnt down in 1594, but was rebuilt at public expense and later used
as a school (Michelet 2, note 2).

[10] CR **6**:156. Cp T.M.Lindsay, *Luther and the German Reformation* (Edinburgh: T.& T.Clark, 1900), 13.

[11] WA Br **1**:610 = LW **48**:145 (Luther to Spalatin, 14 January 1520).

[12] Atkinson 17; Erikson 50. However, as Brecht points out, Hans Luther's economic progress was not without its setbacks and it would be false to describe him as 'a coolly calculating, early modern, small businessman' (Brecht **1**:6).

[13] Brecht **1**:10 and plate I.

[14] Atkinson 18.

[15] Smith 190; WA Br **5**:349 (Luther to Link, 5 June 1530).

[16] Brecht **1**:8.

[17] Luther could have been as young as 4½ years when he entered school at Mansfeld, although the customary age for entrance was 7 years. See Schwiebert 111.

[18] Brendler 26. The *Trivium* of the school curriculum of the Middle Ages was so called because it consisted of the three subjects of the lower division of the Seven Liberal Arts, namely Grammar, Rhetoric and Logic.

[19] WA TR **5**:235 no.5571 = LW **54**:457 no.5571.

[20] Mackinnon **1**:11.

[21] Kuiper 25.

[22] Mackinnon **1**:13.

[23] The Brethren of the Common Life were a semi-monastic religious brotherhood within the Roman Catholic Church founded in the Netherlands in the late fourteenth century. They set up schools or supplied teachers for existing schools (as in the case of Magdeburg) throughout the Netherlands, Germany and Switzerland, and did much to raise the standard of education and piety in these countries before the Reformation. Luther mentions that he was at school with the 'Null Brethren' or *Nullbrüder*s he calls them. Their name was derived from the word *nolle*, the name for the type of cowl which they wore. See WA Br **2**:563 (Luther to Sturm, 15 June 1522) and Brecht **1**:16.

[24] So N.Davies, *Europe: A History* (London: Pimlico, 1997) 486. See Haile 53; WA TR **1**:86 no.194 & **2**:518 no.2545ab.

[25] WA **30**:576 = LW **46**:250. When he was accused by his opponents in 1520 of being a Bohemian and an unorthodox foreigner, Luther replied that nearly all his kinsfolk were to be found in Eisenach and there was no town in which he was better known (WA Br **1**:610 = LW **48**:145; WA TR **5**:76 no.5347. Cp Brecht **1**:17).

[26] WA Br **1**:610 = LW **48**:145 (Luther to Spalatin, 14 January 1520). Cp WA TR **5**:76 no.5347. Georg Spalatin (1484-1545) was chaplain and librarian at the court of Frederick the Wise, the Elector of Saxony. He was a fellow student of Luther at Erfurt and became his great friend and supporter who maintained a voluminous correspondence with him (Sears 47).

[27] Brecht **1**:19; Schwiebert 127. The Victorian novel, *Chronicles of the Schönberg-Cotta Family* by Mrs Rundle Charles (London: Thomas Nelson,

1868) provides an authentic account of the life of the Schalbe-Cotta family, according to Rupp & Drewery 180.

[28] The family name was variously spelt Lauther, Leuder, Leuther, Luder, Ludher, and Lutter, of which most modern authors prefer the spelling Luder for the surname of the Reformer's father. However, about the year 1518 the Reformer began to sign his name as 'Luther' and this spelling was then adopted by all the members of the other Luther families. The name is said to be derived from the old German name Chlotar or Lothar, a forename meaning 'one who is renowned in battle' (Köstlin 2. Cp Oberman 86 and Schwiebert 102).

[29] For an account of the course of study which Luther would follow at Erfurt see Brecht **1**:32-38. The greatest part of his time there would have been spent on logic and its formal structure. It was to this study that Luther 'owed the precision and methodological training of his intellectual power' which he used to such effect in his later life and work (*Ibidem* **1**:38).

[30] Brecht **1**:33-34. Luther so impressed his friends and fellow students with his learning and ability that they nicknamed him The Philosopher (*Philosophus*). Because of his musical ability he was also called The Musician (*Musicus*). See Kuiper 64.

[31] Brecht **1**:48; WA TR **4**:440 no.4707.

[32] The works of the Roman comic writer Plautus were used to acquaint students with colloquial Latin in contrast to the more formal monastic Latin of the schools (Sears 17). At this time Luther did not possess a Bible. He had seen one in the university library at Erfurt and had taken it up at that time and read the story of Hannah and Samuel in First Samuel 1-3 (Sears 48; WA TR **5**:75 no.5346). He only came to possess one when he received a Latin Bible bound in red morocco when he became a novitiate in the monastery (WA TR **1**:44 no.116 = LW **54**:13 no.116). See Brecht **1**:85; Michelet 6, note 1.

[33] The monastery was called the Black Cloister from the black habit worn by the monks of the Augustinian Order. For details of their dress see Brecht **1**:63. In 1945 during the Second World War, this monastery was bombed in an air raid. The cloister was partly destroyed, including the cell which Luther had occupied, but the building has now been restored (Atkinson 57, note 1).

[34] Luther never explained why, amongst the numerous monasteries in Erfurt, he chose to enter that of the Augustinian Eremites, although it was conveniently situated near his university college (Brecht **1**:51). The mendicant Order of the Augustinian Eremites (or Austin Friars) was then the most important monastic Order in Germany and was known for its severe discipline and the rigid enforcement of its Rule. The Order was named after St Augustine (AD 354-430) but its Rule was not drawn up by him, although it was compiled from his writings. The Order was formed in 1256 by the union of eight minor Orders and by the fifteenth century it had over two thousand monasteries in Europe with a central office in Rome. The monks ceased to be hermits soon after the

Order was formed, but nevertheless the name Eremites continued to be used. See Brecht **1**:52-55; Jacobs 23; Köstlin 33.

[35]   Atkinson 57, note 1.

[36]   Boehmer 51. Cp Schwiebert 605.

[37]   Brecht **1**:107; Boehmer 49. Wittenberg was devastated in the Napoleonic wars and when the town was rebuilt, the university was not restored but transferred to Halle and united with the university there under the title of the University of Halle-Wittenberg.

[38]   Smith 2.

[39]   Oberman 278. Cp Kuiper 31 and Marius 24.

[40]   Kuiper 17. Kuiper quotes the description by the Swiss Reformer, John Kessler, from the latter's book *Sabbata* published in 1522 as a chronicle of the persons and events of his time. Kessler had been a student with Luther at Wittenberg. For a fuller account of Kessler's description of Luther and his accidental meeting with Luther disguised as Junker Georg (Squire George) see Freytag 74-82.

[41]   WA Br **1**:525-527 = LW **48**:69 (Luther to Staupitz, 30 May 1518), note 26. Johann von Staupitz (1468-1524) was the first dean of the theological faculty at Wittenberg and Luther's predecessor in the chair of biblical theology. He was appointed vicar-general of the Augustinian Eremites in 1503 and as such he was Luther's superior in his Order. He was Luther's teacher, friend and patron who played a very important part in promoting his career (Rupp 365a).

[42]   Oberman 326. Cp Rupp & Drewery 35 (Peter Mosellanus to Julius Pflug, December 7th 1519). Mosellanus was the professor of Greek at Leipzig University who gave the opening address at the Leipzig Disputation in 1519. Schwiebert (393) calls him professor of Poetry.

[43]   The earliest printed version of the speech Luther made before the Diet of Worms was published in Wittenberg in 1521. It contained the words 'Here I stand, I can do no other. So help me God, Amen (*Hie stehe ich; Ich kann nicht anders thun. Gott helfe mir, Amen)*'. These words were printed in Luther's native German, while the speech was delivered in Latin. However, the words do not appear in the official record made at the time. Nevertheless, they may well be genuine because those listening to the speech were so moved by it, that they did not record all the words Luther said. See Atkinson 202, note 1; Bainton 185; Brendler 206. Cp WA **7**:838.

[44]   Haile 49. Not only was Luther the most prolific author of Germany in his time; he was also the most popular, for the intense interest in the subjects about which he wrote and the forthright and picturesque style in which he wrote about them, ensured a ready market for his writings (Freytag 42).

[45]   Rupp 365b. Cp E.G.Rupp, *Luther's Progress to the Diet of Worms* (London: SCM Press, 1951), 24. Luther's great devotion to biblical study and exposition is illustrated by his remark about the epistle of Paul to the Galatians when he said, 'This is my own dear epistle, to which I am married.

It is my Katie von Bora'. (WA TR **1**:69 no.146 = LW **54**:20 no.146). It was, of course, out of his study and exposition of the Bible that the inspiration arose which produced the Reformation.

[46]   The year 1514 is that given for the Tower experience by Schwiebert 288. However, the editors of the American translation of Luther's works say that it occurred 'at an undetermined date between 1508 and 1518' (See LW **54**:193, note 65). Richard Marius, in his more recent biography of Luther, dates this experience to 1519, or perhaps the winter of 1519-20 (See Marius 203).

[47]   WA TR **3**:228 no.3232c = LW **54**:193 no.3232c and WA TR **4**:72 no.4007 = LW **54**:209 no.4007. 'No matter how much the conception of Luther making his reformatory discovery while on the privy may accord with the fantasies of polemicists, psychologists, and even theologians, it is really much more   probable that he attained his insight at his desk while about his exegetical work' (Brecht **1**:227). Cp Erikson 198.

[48]   Rupp & Drewery 6.

[49]   Schwiebert 576-578.

[50]   Schwiebert 571-573. See Manns *passim* for colour reproductions of the portraits of the years 1520, 1521 and 1528.

[51]   Schwiebert 576.

[52]   *Ibidem* 576.

[53]   *Ibidem* 577.

[54]   Rupp & Drewery 36 (Letter of Peter Mosellanus to Julius Pflug, 17 Dec. 1519).

[55]   Panel 108.

[56]   WA TR **2**:613 no.2176b.

[57]   Davies 43. Cp H.Boehmer, *Luther in the Light of Recent Research* (New York: The Christian Herald, 1916), 213, where the author points out that 'Luther never says that he had been intoxicated, and no one ever saw him drunk, otherwise we would surely know about it, for if ever a man lived in a glasshouse it was Luther'.

[58]   Bornkamm 411; Brecht **3**:240; WA TR **4**:670 no.5117. Seberger had been taken on by Luther in 1517 when Luther found him without any means of livelihood (Köstlin 467).

[59]   Brecht **1**:6.

[60]   This book was published in London by Faber & Faber in 1958.

[61]   Bainton RH in Johnson 23. Erikson (47) admits 'there are only a few facts about Luther's childhood', but nevertheless he proceeds to draw some far-reaching conclusions from them. John Osborne, the British playwright, based his play *Luther* (published by Faber & Faber in 1961) on Erikson's book, but neither Erikson nor he 'understand Luther's great work or his profound experience of grace' (Davies 47).

[62]   Rupp & Drewery 65. Papal documents of this kind are called *bulls* because of the lead seal or *bulla* attached to them and are named from their first words.

[63]   Haile 33.

[64]   These were the conditions identified by the Jesuit scholar Hartmann Grisar in his six-volume biography of Luther, and the Danish psychiatrist, Paul J Reiter in the second volume of his work entitled *Martin Luthers Umwelt, Charackter und Psychose* (Copenhagen: Leven & Munksgaard, 1937-41). Reiter's work is open to criticism on three counts. First, he attributed certain aspects of Luther's personality and behaviour to psychiatric causes, when they could equally well be due to physical causes. Second, he failed to grasp the essential nature of Luther's spiritual experiences. And third, he was unable to understand Luther's theology (Davies 42-43).

[65]   Davies 43.

[66]   Brecht **3**:138; WA TR **3**:344 no.3476 = LW **54**:207 no.3476.

[67]   Davies 44. Cp Bornkamm 557. The physical element in the causation of Luther's episodes of depression is shown on a careful examination of Luther's medical history which reveals that 'in each instance a physical illness precipitated a period of psychological depression... which lasted two or three days at the most' (Spitz LW in Johnson 63). Most often these periods were associated with attacks of renal colic.

[68]   This word *anfechtung* which Luther uses to describe his episodes of spiritual crisis is usually left untranslated in the modern biographies as it is a word which 'defies expression in English'. It is the German equivalent of the Latin *tentatio* and may mean 'trials sent by God or it may refer to the temptations of Satan' (Brecht **1**:x). For a discussion of the theological aspect of the *anfechtungen* see Brecht **1**:76-82.

[69]   WA Br **3**:53 (Luther to Link, 8 April 1523). Cp Brecht **2**:195-201.

[70]   Smith 179. With his marriage to Katharine in 1525, Luther effectively ceased to be a monk since one of the vows he took when he became a monk was that of celibacy. He had already abandoned his cowl in October of the previous year. See Brecht **2**:95.

[71]   Oberman 278. Cp Kuiper 31.

[72]   Jacobs 395-396; Smith 355. It is through Paul and his four sons that most of the branches of the Luther family now trace their descent from the Reformer (Sears 341).

[73]   Smith 181; Brecht **3**:235. Cp WA TR **4**:568 no.5493 = LW **54**:429 no.5493, note 6.

[74]   WA TR **1**:46 no.119 = LW **54**:14 no.119. Cp Panel 108.

[75]   Köstlin 31 & 198. The friends of Luther who visited him in the various inns at which he lodged on his way to the Diet of Worms in April 1521 found him playing his lute as he relaxed in face of the great danger which lay before him, as he believed that he might not return alive from the Diet. See T.M.Lindsay, *History of the Reformation* (Edinburgh: T.& T.Clark, 1909), **1**:273.

[76]   WA TR **1**:150 no.360 = LW **54**:53 no.360.

[77]   WA TR **3**:578 no.3733 = LW **54**:266 no.3733.

[78] WA TR **3**:627 no.3801 = LW **54**:277 no.3801.

[79] WA TR **1**:150 no.360 = LW **54**:53 no.360. Cp A.C.McGiffert, *Martin Luther: The Man and His Work* (London: Fisher Unwin, 1911), 370.

[80] Brecht **2**:204-205. The oaken doors of the Castle Church which are referred to in this paragraph were destroyed by fire in 1760 during a bombardment of Wittenberg. They were replaced in 1812 by doors of bronze on which Luther's Ninety-five Theses were cast (Jacobs 409).

[81] Köstlin 12. This incident is recorded by Dr Ratzeberger in his biography of Luther. For the suggestion that the illness was rheumatic fever see Panel 108. We have no knowledge of any childhood infections in Luther's case but we know that they occurred in his time. For example, he writes in a letter of December 1544 that Margaret and all her brothers have had measles (*morbilli*). All her brothers soon recovered but Margaret ran a high and persistent temperature which had lasted for almost ten weeks when Luther wrote. See WA Br **10**:554 = LW **50**:246 (Luther to Propst, 5 December 1544). There is no indication of the cause of this continued fever but Margaret did eventually recover from it and lived until 1570, when she died at the early age of 36 years.

[82] Smith 379.

[83] For a brief discussion of fever in the sixteenth century see J.Wilkinson, *Proc. R. Coll. Physicians Edin.*, (1992) **22**:375-376. See pages 68-69 of this present volume.

[84] WA Br **4**:137 (Luther to Spalatin, 25 April 1523). For the details of the medical report and its misinterpretation see Grisar **2**:161-164.

[85] WA Br **5**:60 (Luther to Amsdorf, 4 May 1529).

[86] Brecht **3**:231; WA Br **9**:376 (Luther to Melanchthon, 4 April 1541).

[87] WA Br **5**:125 (Luther to Briessmann, 31 July 1529). He calls the sickness 'that English plague (*pestis illa Anglica*)'.

[88] The English Sweat or Sweating Sickness was a communicable disease which ravaged England in five separate epidemics during the period 1485 to 1551 and then disappeared, never to return. It was a short-term fever of high and rapid mortality. The worst epidemic occurred in 1528 and in the following year the infection spread by ship to Hamburg and then rapidly through Germany and other countries, visiting Wittenburg on its way. Its precise nature has never been determined. The absence of respiratory symptoms would seem to exclude influenza which has been a popular identification in the past. A recent suggestion identifies it as an acute encephalitis due to an arbovirus carried by insects from small mammals (voles and mice) which form the primary hosts. See J.A.H.Wylie & L.H.Collier, 'The English Sweating Sickness (*Sudor Anglicus*): A Reappraisal' in *J Hist Med* (1981), **36**:425-445 and also R.E.McGrew, *Encyclopaedia of Medical History*. (London: Macmillan, 1985) 106-108, art. 'English Sweating Sickness'. A full account of this sickness will be found in C.Creighton, *A History of Epidemics in Britain* (Cambridge: Cambridge University Press, 1894), **1**:236-281.

89   WA Br **5**:125 (Luther to Briessman, 31 July 1529). Cp Köstlin 330 and Brecht **2**:210.

90   Brecht **2**:207-209; Smith 188.

91   WA Br **7**:348 = LW **50**:126 (Luther to Müller, 19 January 1536). Cp LW **50**:108, note 11 and Smith 328.

92   Brecht **2**:207-208. WA TR **5**:193 no.5503 = LW **54**:434 no.5503.

93   WA Br **2**:298 = LW **48**:197 (Luther to Spalatin, 14 April 1521). Cp Rupp & Drewery 30 and WA Br **1**:209 (Luther to Spalatin, 10 October 1518). See also Boehmer 233.

94   Brecht **3**:23; WA Br **7**:245 = LW **50**:87 (Luther to Melanchthon, 29 Aug. 1535).

95   WA TR **3**:6 no.3912 = LW **54**:293 no.3912.

96   Manns 115.

97   WA Br **5**:544 = LW **49**:400 (Luther to his wife, 14 August 1530).

98   WA Br **4**:221 (Luther to Spalatin, 10 July 1527), note 3. Cp WA TR **3**:138 no.3006a = LW **54**:189 no.3006a. For a detailed discussion (in German) of the possibility that Luther suffered from Ménière's syndrome which finally concludes that he did, see H.Feldmann, 'Martin Luther's seizure disorder' in *Sudhoffs Arch Z Wissenschaftsgesch* (1989) **73**(1):26-44. See also Panel 107.

99   Brecht **2**:203.

100   Brecht **2**:374; WA Br **11**:269 = LW **50**:284 (Luther to his wife, 25 Jan. 1546).

101   WA Br **11**:263 (Luther to Propst, 17 January 1546). Luther's reference to being 'one-eyed (*monoculus*)' suggests he was now suffering from cataract in one eye (Panel 109). Mackinnon, however, suggests he had an acute eye infection at this time but gives no evidence for this suggestion (Mackinnon **4**:209, note 16). The eye affected appears to have been the left one according to the additional material collected in WA Br **13**:351. Cp LW **50**:284-285 notes 1 & 2.

102   Brecht **1**:472; Boehmer 427; WA Br **2**:337 = LW **48**:227-228 (Luther to Spalatin 14 May 1521); WA Tr **5**:82 no.5353. In his letter to Spalatin, written ten days after he arrived at the Wartburg, he complains that 'I sit here all day long drunk with leisure (*otiosus et crapulosus*)', but that leisure did not last very long for he soon took up his pen to write letters and treatises, and to translate the Greek New Testament.

103   WA TR **6**:208 no.6815. Cp Bornkamm 1-2. Luther called the Wartburg 'my Patmos' in an allusion to the banishment of the apostle John to the Greek island of Patmos referred to in Revelation 1:9. Luther was, in fact, quite familiar with his new surroundings at the Wartburg for he had spent part of his childhood at Eisenach, and he recalled having picked strawberries at the castle as a child. See WA TR **5**: 82 no. 5353 and Marius 297.

104   Bornkamm 257: 'Not until 9 October 1524, did he preach for the first time without his cowl. On October 16th he wore it again for the morning service, but for the last time; at the afternoon service he appeared without it.' See WA TR **4**:303 no.4414 = LW **54**:337-338 no.4414.

[105] WA Br **2**:357 = LW **48**:257 (Luther to Melanchthon, 13 July 1521). Cp Rupp & Drewery 73, note 1.

[106] See, for instance, WA Br **2**:334 = LW **48**:218 (Luther to Amsdorf 12 May 1521).

[107] WA Br **2**:334 = LW **48**:219 (Luther to Melanchthon, 12 May 1521).

[108] WA Br **2**:368 = LW **48**:276 (Luther to Spalatin, 31 July 1521).

[109] WA Br **2**:378 = LW **49**:291 (Luther to Spalatin, 6 August 1521).

[110] WA Br **2**:365 = LW **48**:268 (Luther to Spalatin, 15 July 1521).

[111] WA Br **2**:395 = LW **48**:316 (Luther to Spalatin, 7 October 1521).

[112] CR **1**:801 (Melanchthon to Lang, 24 June 1526).

[113] Brecht **3**:23. The occurrence of renal colic followed by the passage of several small stones suggests that these were uric acid or urate stones which had originated in the kidney (See Panel 111).

[114] Haile 213; WA Br **8**:40 (Luther to Jonas, 9 February 1537).

[115] Brecht **3**:185; Köstlin 407. Luther said that as the people of old stoned Stephen (See Acts 7:58) so now he was being 'stoned' by his stone! Schwiebert describes this condition as a 'severe attack of gallstones' (580 & 599), but the occurrence of urinary obstruction clearly indicates that the stones originated in the kidney and not in the gall-bladder.

[116] WA TR **3**:578 no.3733 = LW **54**:266 no.3733.

[117] Luther appears to have had a high opinion of preparations from the *Faecal Pharmacopoeia*. Preparations from pig faeces were used to promote blood flow; from horse faeces to relieve chest pain; and human faeces were applied to wounds (Brecht **2**:429-430; WA Br **6**:165 (Luther to Link, 18 August 1531); WA TR **2**:301 no.2040.

[118] WA Br **8**:50 = LW **50**:167 (Luther to his wife, 27 February 1537).

[119] Brecht **3**:185; WA TR **3**:389 no.3543a = LW **54**:226 no.3543a and WA TR **3**:578 no.3733 = LW **54**:266 no.3733.

[120] Brecht **3**:187; WA Br 8:51 = LW **50**:167 (Luther to his wife, 27 February 1537). Note 4 to the German original of this letter gives the metric equivalent of one *Stübig* as about three to four litres or six Imperial pints.

[121] WA Br **8**:54 (Melanchthon to Luther, 27 February 1537), note 3. Cp LW **50**:168 note 22. See also CR **3**:270 (Melanchthon to Jonas, 23 February 1537) and Smith 312-313. This farewell document is addressed to his family and friends and is commonly called his first will. He drew up his second and more formal will in 1542. Unfortunately, because of his dislike of lawyers, Luther did this without the help of a notary as required by law, and after his death his will was declared invalid by the unfriendly Court Chancellor of Electoral Saxony, Dr Gregory Brück, with the result that although Luther had left a considerable fortune, it was mostly used up in legal fees as Katie contested the actions and decisions of the Chancellor against her during the imprisonment of the friendly Elector John Frederick by the Emperor Charles V, after his defeat at the Battle of Mühlenburg in April 1547. Katie was obliged to support herself and her family by taking paying guests into their home in the

monastery. She died on 20 December 1552, three months after a road accident sustained when she was fleeing from the plague which had broken out in Wittenberg. She was buried in St Mary's Church, Torgau (Smith 424-426).

122 Haile 220; WA TR **3**:304 no.3395c.

123 Brecht 3:229; WA TR **3**:491 no.3655a.

124 Haile 329.

125 WA Br **11**:131 = LW **50**:265 (Luther to Amsdorf, 9 July 1545). Luther had previously spoken of 'my enemy, the stone (*hostis meus calculus*)' in WA Br **8**:219 = LW **50**:179 (Luther to Edward Fox on 12 May 1538). Fox was the Bishop of Hereford in England and he gave Luther some helpful advice about the treatment of the attacks of his stone during a visit to Wittenberg in 1536. Others of his friends sent him their favourite remedies. For example, the Protestant Duke Albrecht of Prussia sent him a supply of white amber, which Luther used in a mixture made up with specially-powdered fish bones (Brecht **3**:232).

126 WA Br **11**:300 = LW **50**:312 (Luther to his wife, 2 February 1546).

127 WA TR **4**:334 no.4479 = LW **54**:346 no.4479.

128 WA TR **3**:292 no.3365.

129 Brecht **3**:230.

130 Brecht **3**: Plate III which is a photograph of the plaster casts of Luther's hands now on display in the *Staatliche Lutherhalle* in Wittenberg.

131 WA TR **3**:537 no.3693. The origin of Luther's gout and renal stones has been traced to his stay in the Wartburg where the combination of a sedentary life-style and a high-purine diet might have been responsible for the production of the renal stones. See G.F.H.Kürchenmeister, *Dr Martin Luthers Krankengeschichte* (Leipzig: 1881), 41 and Reiter, op. cit. **2**:32 (in Ref.64 above). Cp Bornkamm 553. However, it should be noted that five years elapsed between his time in the Wartburg and the first appearance of symptoms suggestive of renal stones in 1526.

132 WA Br **7**:379 (Luther to Bucer, 25 March 1536). See also Brecht **3**:23 and WA Br **7**:372 (Luther to Hausman, 11 March 1536).

133 WA **44**:825 = LW **8**:333. We have accepted the emendation of the Weimar editors who suggested the words 'the book (*der liber*)' should be read instead of 'the dear (*der liebe*)'.

134 Brecht **3**:370.

135 For details of the dispute see LW **50**:281-283. Cp Brecht **3**:369-370. Rupp (371b) describes the two Counts of Mansfeld who were involved in the dispute as 'arrogant young princes'!

136 WA Br **11**:277 = LW **50**:294 (Luther to Melanchthon, 1 February 1546). The phrase *humor ventriculi* describes a sensation resembling the movement of fluid within the heart chambers and is appropriately translated as 'palpitations' in modern clinical terms. See LW **50**:294, note 14.

137 WA Br **11**:291 (See note 3) = LW **50**:305-306 (Luther to his wife, 10 February 1546).

[138] WA TR **6**:302 no.6975. Cp Köstlin 489. This saying was one of the last to be recorded in Luther's *Table Talk*. It was written down by John Aurifaber (Goldsmith) of Weimar, the last of Luther's amanuenses, at Eisleben on February 16th 1547. The dispute which had brought Luther to Eisleben proved to be far from settled by the agreements signed on 16 and 17 February, and further controversy broke out within weeks of Luther's death (Brecht **3**:374).

[139] Brecht **3**:375; Michelet 350.

[140] The horn of the traditional unicorn was in reality the spiral tusk of the narwhal or sea-unicorn (*Monodon monoceros*). This is an Arctic toothed-whale characterised in the male by a long horn-like tusk which is the the whale's left upper tooth and may project forwards for some nine feet from the upper jaw. Gratings from this tusk taken in wine were believed to be an effective antidote against poison and a certain cure for plague and malignant fevers. See A.C.Wootton, *Chronicles of Pharmacy* (London: Macmillan, 1910), **1**:29.

[141] Brecht **3**:376.

[142] Köstlin 490-491.

[143] Brecht **3**:375-376. Cp Köstlin 489-491. It is said that more details are known of the death of Martin Luther than of any other event in history (Schwiebert 747). Fourteen eye-witnesses were present at his bedside when he died and afterwards they prepared a certified document which was printed and published in Wittenberg a few months later. Also a number of those present published their individual accounts of his death in the form of letters, sermons or reports. The most reliable of these was prepared by Luther's colleagues Justus Jonas and Michael Coelius, and included also the details of his burial (See WA **54**:478-496). For the bibliographical details of these accounts see Mackinnon **4**:210, note 20 and Schwiebert 876, note 20.

[144] It was later alleged that the troops of the Holy Roman Emperor Charles V had desecrated Luther's grave and scattered its contents when they sacked Wittenberg in March 1547. However, when the Castle Church was restored in 1892 the grave was opened and the coffin found to be well-preserved with its contents intact (Schwiebert 752 & 878, note 66).

[145] CR **11**:726-734 (Melanchthon's eulogy at the funeral of Luther at Wittenberg on 22 February 1546). Cp CR **6**:80 (Melanchthon to Camerarius, 21 March 1546) and Brecht **3**:378-380.

[146] Grisar **6**:380. The report from which Grisar quotes was written by Johann Landau, the town apothecary of Eisleben, who was not an eyewitness of Luther's death, but was called in immediately after Luther had died, in order to give him an enema. This report is not regarded as very trustworthy for it does not always agree with the testimony of those who were eyewitnesses of his death (Schwiebert 876, note 20). The significance of his observation that the whole of the right side of Luther's body was dusky and discoloured (*infuscatus*) is not clear. The physician who thought that Luther had died

from apoplexy appears to have regarded this discoloration as supporting his diagnosis. If this were so, it would mean that Luther had sustained a left-sided cerebrovascular accident which could also have affected his speech. On the other hand, such discoloration is not recognised today as a manifestion of apoplexy or hemiplegia. Also, the observation was made only a very short time after death when it was unlikely that any postmortem discoloration would have begun to appear. It appears that we must leave the significance of the observation unexplained clinically.

[147] CR **6**:58 (Melanchthon's announcement to Luther's students on 19 February of his death the previous day). This opinion of Melanchthon's that Luther's death was due to a natural cause was presumably based on his knowledge of Luther's previous medical history (see Reference 136 above), on the observations of the eye-witnesses who were present during his final heart attack, and on the reports of two local physicians who were called in to attend Luther just before he died. It was an opinion which was at first accepted by both Luther's friends and enemies alike. However, about twenty years after his death, rumours began to be circulated by his enemies which alleged that he had died from some unspeakable disease contracted in the course of immoral behaviour, or alternatively that he had in fact committed suicide by hanging himself from his bed frame or by his deliberate ingestion of some poisonous substance (see Grisar **6**:381-386). None of these rumours are probable in themselves, and cannot be substantiated from the eye-witness accounts we have of the circumstances surrounding Luther's death. They can only be explained by the desire of their originators to dishonour the Reformer's memory and besmirch his character. For a recent discussion of the circumstances of Luther's death and the reports which afterwards circulated about it, see Michael B.Lukens, 'Luther's death and the Secret Catholic Report' in the *Journal of Theological Studies* (1991) **41**:545-553.

[148] Brecht **2**:205-207; WA Br **4**:160 (Luther to Spalatin, 13 January 1527). The plant *Carduus benedictus* (the blessed thistle) is also known as *Geum urbanum* (wood avens or herb bennet). It got its name from the belief that it possessed extraordinary medicinal powers in cases of plague, malignant fevers, poisoning and even cancer. It was also used in cases of precordial pain, and hence this watery extract of the plant was sometimes called 'benedictine heart water' (Bornkamm 554), a name which has no connection with the monastic Order of St Benedict. The reputation of this plant was quite unjustified and extracts of the leaves or seeds of the plant eventually came to be used in pharmacy as a simple bitter. See W.Woodville, *Medical Botany* (London: James Phillips, Printer, 1790), **1**:119-121.

[149] WA Br **4**:222 = LW **49**:169 (Luther to Hausmann, 13 July 1527), note 10. Cp Köstlin 303-304.

[150] WA TR **1**:74 no.157 = LW **54**:23 no.157. The reference to urinoscopy should be noted. Cp WA TR **4**:6 no.3912 = LW **54**:294 no.3912.

[151] Brecht **3**:23; WA TR **2**:119 no.3510 = LW **54**:218 no.3510 and WA TR **5**:475 no.6079.

[152] WA TR **4**:8 no.3916 = LW **54**:294 no.3916. Luther had apparently been in the habit of counting his pulse beats. See Haile 33 and WA TR **2**:187 no.1699.

[153] Sears 337; Bornkamm 554.

[154] Hypertension would not be the only result of the damage to the kidney due to the presence of stones, for this would also produce some degree of failure of renal function. We have already seen how with the prolonged obstruction to the outflow of urine at Schmalkalden in February 1537, the symptoms of acute uraemia began to appear. It is possible that Luther's irritability and inability to remember and concentrate in the last few years of his life may have been due to chronic renal failure (Davies 42-43).

[155] Köstlin 198.

[156] WA Br **2**:298 = LW **48**:198 (Luther to Spalatin, 14 April 1521), note 2.

[157] Brecht **2**:205; WA Br **3**:418 (Luther to Briessmann, 11 January 1525).

[158] According to Haile (19 & 33), Luther suffered from phlebitis of his left leg and it was the periodic opening of a vein in the resultant varicose ulcer which provided the *fontanella*.

[159] Brecht **3**:231.

[160] WA Br **11**:291 (Luther to his wife, 10 February 1546), note 10. Bluestone or crude copper sulphate was formerly used as a caustic to remove excessive granulation tissue produced during the healing of ulcers and burns.

[161] WA Br **10**:374 (Dorothy, Countess of Mansfeld to Luther, 26 August 1543). Cp LW **50**:305, note 14 and Brecht **3**:231-232.

[162] WA Br **11**:301 = LW **50**:314 (Luther to Melanchthon, 14 February 1546).

[163] This was also the diagnosis of the Chicago medical panel. See Panel 116.

Chapter 2

THE MEDICAL HISTORY OF JOHN CALVIN

The medical history of John Calvin, the Genevan Reformer, does not figure at all prominently in the standard accounts of his life.[1] These set out the achievements of Calvin in face of the political, social and ecclesiastical difficulties he had to encounter and overcome, and there is no doubt that these difficulties were considerable. However, his achievements are all the more remarkable when seen against the background of his personal medical history, in so far as this is known in any detail.

The fact that so little is known is due to Calvin's 'customary brevity in autobiography' to quote the phrase of one of his modern biographers.[2] Another puts this brevity more in context when he writes that 'Calvin was by nature uncommunicative about his personal history; a certain timidity, an aristocratic inclination to screen himself from the public, and finally his conviction that the individual is nothing in himself but only in so far as he is an instrument of the Divine will, caused him to remain silent about many events that would have interested biographers'.[3] The result was that Calvin was the most self-effacing of all the religious leaders of the Reformation, always reluctant to speak about himself and his own experiences. We can however glean something of his medical history from his own letters and from the writings of his friends and colleagues.

The Sources

We are fortunate in having three accounts of Calvin's life written soon after his death by two men who were his close associates in Geneva. Two of these accounts were written in French. The first one was by Theodore Beza (1519-1605), his colleague and successor, and was published a few weeks after his death in May 1564 to accompany the posthumous publication of Calvin's commentary on the book of Joshua. The second appeared in the following year. It was longer and more detailed and was written by Nicolas Colladon, who had succeeded Calvin in the chair of theology in the College of Geneva.

In 1575 Beza published the third biography. This time it was in Latin and more than twice the length of his previous one written in French. All three of these biographies include incidental references to Calvin's health, although not as many as we might have wished. The more productive source of medical detail about Calvin is to be found in his own letters. His correspondence was voluminous and a great number of his letters have survived. These letters deal with an astonishing variety of subjects and sometimes reveal details of the state of his health at the time he wrote them. These details may be revealed in explanation of his delay in answering his correspondents' letters, or may occur in brief reports on his health made to his close friends, who from time to time expressed concern about him and the state of his health.

Amongst his letters is one which is of great medical interest for it is virtually a medical report on his health written by Calvin himself in the last year of his life. Calvin noticed that his doctor at that time, Philibert Sarrazin, had changed his treatment and when he asked the reason for this change, Dr Sarrazin said that he had received advice from the members of the Medical Faculty of Montpellier who had expressed concern about Calvin's health. The result was that Calvin wrote to them to thank them for their concern and set out the details of his medical history for their information, albeit in his usual brief fashion. This letter was dated 8 February 1564, four months before he died.[4]

Family History

John Calvin was born in the cathedral city of Noyon in Picardy about sixty miles north-east of Paris, in the afternoon of Tuesday 10 July 1509. He was baptised that same month in the parish church of St Godebert, being given the name of John after his godfather, John de Vatines, one of the canons of Noyon cathedral. In former times, Noyon had been a city of some importance for it was there that Charlemagne had been crowned king of the western Frankish kingdom of Neustria (Central Gaul) in 768 and Hugh Capet crowned king of France in 987. However, by the sixteenth century the city had lost much of its civil and ecclesiastical importance.

John was the second of six children born to Gérard Cauvin[5] and his wife Jeanne Lefranc. Four of these children were boys and two were girls.[6] One of the boys, François, died in childhood. Their mother was noted for her religious devotion, her remarkable beauty and her motherly affection,[7] but she died in 1515 when John was only six years old, with the result that she is not mentioned in any of his writings.[8] After his wife's death, her husband married again but the name of his second wife who was a widow, is not known. She bore him another two daughters.

Gérard's ancestors had been boatmen or coopers at Pont l'Evêque, a small fishing village on the river Oise, a tributary of the Seine, about two miles from Noyon. Early in his life, Gérard had left the family home to seek advancement in Noyon. By at least the year 1481, he had established himself as a successful advocate there[9] and he became a shrewd man of business who eventually held both ecclesiastical and civil offices there. In 1497 he was admitted a burgess of the city and about the same time married his first wife, the daughter of another Noyon burgess, a well-to-do innkeeper who had retired there from Cambrai and come to live as a near neighbour to Gérard Cauvin in the Place au Blé in Noyon.[10]

Although Gérard was secretary of the diocese, he was in no sense a member of the clergy, but was wholly concerned with its secularities. Latterly, his relationships with the Church authorities deteriorated and he was accused of careless accounting in connection with the estates of two deceased priests for whom he had been appointed executor, with the result that on 13 November 1528 he was excommunicated by the local Cathedral Chapter.[11] On 26 May 1531, when he was then about seventy-five years of age, he died at Noyon following an illness lasting some weeks, the nature of which is unknown. He was still under the ban of the Church when he died. However, on the intercession of Charles, his eldest son, he was granted posthumous absolution and allowed Christian burial in consecrated ground.[12]

Charles Cauvin was a priest at the village of Roupy and in the previous February, he had himself been excommunicated for his violent conduct towards the staff of Noyon cathedral, to which an accusation of heresy was later added. On his deathbed in October 1537, he was offered absolution and the Church's last rites, but he refused them and was buried in unconsecrated ground beneath the gallows at Noyon.[13]

From what we know of the good social standing and moderate prosperity of the family, we may presume that John Calvin passed his childhood and early teens in circumstances which provided him with adequate nutrition, clothing, shelter and education. There is no mention of the occurrence of the infectious diseases of childhood which he must have encountered, and safely passed through. The epidemic disease which reached Noyon from time to time and which was often endemic there in the sixteenth century was bubonic plague. This disease had arrived in Europe from the East in the fourteenth century as the Black Death and it was greatly feared by the people because of its high mortality. A particularly virulent outbreak occurred in Noyon in August 1523, when Calvin was fourteen years old. This was probably one reason why his father sent him in that year to Paris to begin his studies at the University there.

Education

He began his formal education in the local Collège des Capettes in Noyon, which was so called from the little capes the scholars wore.[14] This Collège had been founded in 1294 for the education of the children of the poor in Noyon and was situated outside the city wall on the road to Pont l'Evêque. However, Calvin did not stay there long before he went to Paris along with the three sons of the local noble house of de Hangest and its Montmor branch, who had been his boyhood friends. He arrived in Paris in August 1523, and lodged with his Uncle Richard, a locksmith who lived near the large Gothic Church of Saint-Germain-l'Auxerrois beside the Louvre on the Right Bank of the Seine.

To begin with, Calvin received lessons at his uncle's house from a tutor whom he later regarded as incompetent; 'a dull-witted man (*homo stolidus*)' was Calvin's description of him.[15] In August 1523, when he was fourteen years old, he was admitted as a 'martinet' or day-boy to the nearby Collège de la Marche[16], and so became a member of the University of Paris, at that time the most famous educational institution in Europe. However, the academic reputation of this Collège was not very high and its atmosphere was regarded as too liberal for one looking forward to entering the priesthood,[17] and so when he began his Arts course a few months later, he entered the fourteenth century Collège de Montaigu in the Latin quarter of Paris as a resident student. This was a more conservative and more strictly ecclesiastical Collège, which had for long been notorious for its severe discipline, its unhygienic conditions and its poor and insufficient food, as well as the strict orthodoxy of its teaching.[18]

Desiderus Erasmus had entered this Collège thirty years before Calvin and in his book *Ichthyophagia* (A Fish Diet), published in 1526, he describes the conditions there: 'bedding so hard, diet coarse and scanty, sleepless nights and labours so burdensome'. He went on to say that 'I know many who even today cannot shake off the illness they contracted there'. Erasmus said he carried little away from this Collège except a generous supply of lice and fleas.[19] Conditions at the Collège were also commented on by the French satirist, François Rabelais, who speaks of 'that verminous Collège (*ce Collège de pouillerie*)'.[20] Ignatius Loyola, then aged thirty-seven, overlapped with Calvin at the Collège for most of the year 1528, but he left no comments on the conditions he found there. Although Calvin was a paying student he would not be able to escape the insalubrious conditions and oppressive atmosphere of the Collège.

Calvin was fortunate in his teachers at both the colleges he attended. Mathurin Cordier was a distinguished Latin scholar and teacher at the Collège de la Marche who became a life-long friend of Calvin's and ended his days in Geneva at Calvin's invitation. It was probably from him that Calvin acquired 'that unfailing sense of style and diction that marks all his writings'.[21] Beza tells us that at the Collège de Montaigu he continued his Latin studies under a learned Spanish tutor whom he does not name, but has been identified as Antonio Coronel.[22] It is probable that his teachers also included the famous Scottish scholastic philosopher John Mair (or Major), from whom he may have acquired his first real knowledge of Luther's teaching.[23] However, such was the widespread interest in this teaching in both the city and university of Paris that it would have been very difficult for the young Calvin to avoid hearing about its content and nature.[24]

At the end of his Arts course in 1528, Calvin did not proceed to the study of theology as his father had at first intended him to do. Instead, his father now insisted that he should study law and not theology. The reasons usually given for this change are first, his father's quarrel with the local Cathedral Chapter to which we have already referred, and second, his father's view that the study of law was 'a surer road to wealth and honour' than the study of theology.[25] The result was that Calvin enrolled for the course in civil law at the University of Orleans to study under Pierre de l'Estoile, the leading French lawyer at that time. In May 1529 he moved to the more recently founded University of Bourges to attend the lectures of the famous Italian lawyer, Andrea Alciati, who had had joined the faculty of law there in April 1529. Both Calvin's early biographers comment on the reputation for massive industry that he gained at this period and suggest how this affected his health. Colladon says simply that this industry was 'detrimental to his health',[26] whilst Beza is more specific and says that his hard work was responsible not only for his solid learning and excellent memory, but also for 'that weakness of the stomach (*imbecillitas ventriculi*) which afterwards brought on various diseases, and ultimately led to his untimely death'.[27] It may have been whilst he was studying at Bourges that Calvin met Theodore Beza, then aged about ten, who was to become his most intimate friend, his biographer and his successor at Geneva.[28] However, such a meeting was not mentioned in his biography by Beza, who might have been expected to do so, if it had in fact occurred.[29]

After some time, Calvin grew dissatisfied with Alciati's lectures which were very critical of l'Estoile, his former teacher. The result was that in October 1530 he returned to Orleans where he graduated as a licentiate in law (*licencié ès lois*) in February 1531.[30] Soon thereafter he was recalled to Noyon by the terminal illness of his father. After the death of his father on 26 May 1531, Calvin felt himself no longer bound by his promise to him to pursue a legal career and he returned to Paris to pursue the study of literature. In April 1532 he published his first work, a commentary on the *De Clementia* (On Mercy) of the Stoic philosopher Seneca, which established his name as a humanist scholar, although this work was his first and his last purely humanist publication.

It was about this time that Calvin latinised his surname from Cauvin to Calvinus, and on the title page of his commentary on Seneca's work this new form of his surname appeared in print for the first time. In French and English, the name became Calvin.[31]

Calvin had been brought up a devout French Roman Catholic, but during his student days in Paris he became familiar with 'the Lutheran heresy', as the teaching of the Protestant Reformers was called by its opponents. As we have already mentioned, this may have been initially through the lectures of John Major at the Collège de Montaigu. During his legal studies at Bourges around the end of 1529 or the beginning of 1530, he committed himself fully to the Protestant Reformation, the movement to which he was to make so important and long-lasting a contribution.[32]

General Picture of Calvin

Beza describes Calvin as a man 'of moderate stature, of a pale and dark complexion, with eyes that sparkled to the moment of his death, and bespoke his great intellect. In dress he was neither overcareful nor mean, but such as became his singular modesty. In diet he was temperate, being equally averse to penury and luxury'.[33]

The picture of Calvin which emerges from a study of his letters is of a man who suffered from chronic ill health. As early as 1534, when he was twenty-four years old, we find him writing to François Daniel, a fellow student of his days at the universities of Orleans and Bourges, and speaking of his 'constitutional weakness and infirmity of which you are well aware'.[34] Scattered through his letters are numerous references to his bodily weakness, his indolence (due to exhaustion rather than laziness) and the doubtful state of his health.

His life style was a simple one.[35] He rarely had much money and on occasions was reduced to poverty. This was particularly true during his three and a half years in Strasburg. His French congregation there could do little to support him. He lectured three times a week on John's gospel and the Corinthian epistles but received only a florin a week for all his effort.[36] On one occasion he wrote from Strasburg to his friend William Farel saying, 'My present position is such that I do not have a penny'.[37] On another occasion, also in Strasbourg, he had to pledge or sell some of his books in order to pay his landlord and keep himself in food.[38] In an endeavour to make ends meet he took in French students as paying guests, who came to Strasburg to train for the ministry under his guidance. However, these were mostly poor too and could ill afford the two francs a week he expected them to pay for their board and lodging.[39] Even after his return to Geneva in 1541 his stipend was none too large, and he remained a poor man throughout his life. A month before he died, Calvin drew up his will and this shows that his total estate at this time consisted of a silver cup (which had been presented to him two years previously) and a sum of two hundred and twenty-five gold crowns or *écus*.[40]

Marital History

Calvin did not marry until early August 1540 when he was thirty-one, by which time he was pastor of the French-speaking congregation in Strasbourg. His bride was Idelette de Bure, a native of Liège, who is described by Beza as 'a grave and honourable woman'.[41] Her family had been deprived of their property and banished from Belgium in 1533 for their adherence to the Protestant faith. She was the widow of Jean Stordeur, another Belgian refugee, who had died of plague in February 1540 leaving her in poverty with two children, a son and a daughter. Calvin had met her as a member of his Strasbourg congregation. He describes her as 'a woman of rare qualities (*singularis exempli femina*)'.[42] They were married by Farel in Strasbourg, when Calvin at once fell ill with neuralgia and his wife with a fever, which her husband then contracted, bringing their honeymoon to an end after about two weeks.[43]

On 28 July 1542, almost two years after she married Calvin, Idelette was delivered of a son. The delivery was premature and 'not without extreme danger (*non sine extremo periculo*)'.[44] The little boy was baptised and given the name of Calvin's uncle Jacques.[45] To the great distress of his parents he lived only twenty-two days, probably because of his prematurity.

Calvin gives no indication of the nature of the 'extreme danger' to which his wife was exposed during her labour. Since this was premature it is unlikely that the danger arose from any mechanical abnormality of the labour since the child would be small, and she had already borne two children normally. It is more probable that the danger came from her general state of health. At this time she was under the care of Dr Benedict Textor, the Calvin family physician, who was one of the three physicians who practised in Geneva during that period.[46] Calvin mentions that his wife was so ill and weak after the delivery that she was unable to reply to letters, even by dictation.[47]

It is sometimes maintained that his wife bore Calvin two more children who did not survive.[48] However, Calvin appears to deny this when in 1561 he writes in response to the attack on him by François Baudouin, a former secretary, as follows:

> He reproaches me that I am without children. The Lord gave me a little son (*filiolus*), and then he took him away.[49]

Also, in his contemporary biography of Calvin, Nicolas Colladon clearly states that Idelette had only one child by Calvin, and that was a son.[50]

Idelette had been in delicate health when she married Calvin, and she was never really well again after the birth of Jacques. Nevertheless, she proved to be an excellent minister's wife. She visited the poor, sat by the bedside of the sick, entertained his friends, accompanied him on his infrequent walks into the country and assisted at the confinements of the wives of his neighbouring colleagues.[51] However, there are many references in Calvin's letters to his wife's being confined to bed. On one occasion when she had recovered from a serious illness in 1545, he speaks of her as 'a woman brought back to life (*une femme resuscitée*)', indicating how ill she must have been.[52] In August 1548, about six months before she died he speaks of her being in bed with 'a prolonged illness' but he gives no indication of the nature of the illness, which may have been that from which she eventually died.[53]

After only nine years of happy married life with Calvin she died at 8pm on 29 March 1549. In a letter to his friend Pierre Viret, Calvin says that with her death, he has lost 'the excellent companion of my life (*optima socia vitae*)' and 'that while she lived, she was the faithful helper of my ministry. Never did I experience from her the least hindrance'.[54]

Calvin did not marry again and mentions in a sermon on First Timothy that this was because of 'my infirmity (*mon infirmité*)' which meant in his opinion, 'that perhaps a woman might not be happy with me'.[55] As we have already mentioned, about fifteen years previously, he had written about his 'constitutional weakness and infirmity' to his friend François Daniel.[56] Unfortunately, on neither occasion does he define the nature of this infirmity, which presumably means that it was familiar to his audience and to his friend. The two common suggestions are his bad state of health or his irritability. A more specific suggestion which could account for both states, might be that attacks of migraine or hemicrania were the infirmity to which he refers. He mentions these attacks frequently in his letters, and he appears to have suffered from them for most of his life. Whatever its nature may have been, this infirmity meant that he remained a widower for the rest of his life.

Calvin's Personality

As we have already observed, Calvin was shy and reserved and always reluctant to speak about himself, his feelings and his experiences.

His earliest writings and the personal documents which might have shed some light on the formative years of his life have all disappeared. They were presumably confiscated by the police when they searched his room at the Collège de Fortret in Paris in January 1535 for any incriminating evidence against him, after he had fled to escape arrest.[57] His later writings contain few autobiographical references and even these are brief and sometimes difficult to interpret. Consequently, little material now exists on which an adequate and reliable assessment of Calvin's personality may be based.

One result of this has been to allow free rein to authors, both friendly and hostile, to compile and publish their own descriptions of Calvin's personality, many of which lack historical foundation and fail to distinguish fact from fiction. One of the most intensely hostile biographies of Calvin is that by Jerome Bolsec, published in Lyons in 1577. Bolsec was a Carmelite monk and a self-styled physician who had fallen out with Calvin over the subject of predestination. As a result, his biography was concerned only to defame Calvin and present him as an arrogant, malicious and bloodthirsty tyrant who engaged in both heterosexual and homosexual promiscuity, who regarded his words as the word of God and allowed himself to be worshipped as God. This biography is the source of the calumny that Calvin died of syphilis. It is unfortunate that many of the unsubstantiated allegations of this biography have been accepted as fact in modern unsympathetic accounts of the life and actions of Calvin.[58]

Calvin's own assessment of his personality at the end of his life was that he was 'a poor timid scholar (*un pauvre escholier timide*)' and had always been such throughout his life.[59]

That he was a scholar there can be no doubt. The Biblical commentaries and theological treatises which were the products of his scholarship are in print to this day, and are still consulted with profit by modern students and scholars alike. They bear witness to his ability to apply his mind to reading and to study, to the acuity of his intellect and the amazing breadth and depth of his memory.

Of his timidity there can be more doubt for he faced occasions of danger and violence with courage and even bravery. He was never timid when he felt that the will and the honour of God were at stake and the preaching and teaching of the gospel were in jeopardy. When this occurred he sometimes lost his temper, for he admitted that he was 'conscious of possessing a more vehement temper than he would wish'.[60] However, he fully recognises that any outburst of anger dishonours God and needs repentance and forgiveness. In fact, his outbursts of anger may be regarded as reflecting his sensitivity to anything which called into question the truth or the honour of God or his servants, rather than arising from any permanent trait of his character.

No one can understand the personality of Calvin who omits the influence of his Christian faith on his character and behaviour. He was convinced that he had been called by God to the office of pastor and preacher of the gospel of the grace of God revealed in Jesus Christ. This conviction was the source of his authority and the basis of his life and work. It was also the basis of his happiness for, although McGrath suggests that Calvin was an unhappy man, it is the certain knowledge that they are in the line of the will of God and the object of the love of God which is the basis of the Christian believers' happiness and joy. Also, Calvin must have known the happiness and satisfaction of the scholar as he studied the Scriptures and the books in his library, and then as he expounded those same Scriptures to the crowded congregations who came to hear his sermons and lectures from the pulpit and lectern.

There have been two main views of Calvin as a person. The one has been described most recently by McGrath who regards Calvin as 'not a particularly attractive person', as compared with Martin Luther, but one who was 'a somewhat cold and detached individual'.[61] The other view may be stated in the words of Philip Schaff, the Church historian of last century. He wrote that 'nothing can be more unjust than the charge that Calvin was cold and unsympathetic. His whole correspondence proves the reverse. His letters on the death of his wife to his dearest friends reveal a deep fountain of tenderness and affection'.[62]

Factors Affecting Calvin's Health

There are a number of factors which we may identify in Calvin's situation, which may not have been the primary causes of his ill health, but which would readily serve to perpetuate it. These are in addition to his poverty which we have already mentioned.

The *first* is that of subnutrition and even malnutrition. We have already mentioned his experience at the Collège de Montaigu where the students were ill-fed, because of insufficient food and abundant fast-days. Throughout his life he does not appear to have taken an adequate diet. He treated his attacks of migraine and dyspepsia by periods of starvation. In the last ten years or so of his life he existed on only one meal daily, taken in the evening.[63] He never took any food between his meals until, in the last months of his life, his doctors were able to persuade him to take a little wine and a raw egg at midday.[64] A study of the portraits painted of Calvin at the different periods of his life shows an increasing emaciation which may reflect his customary abstemiousness towards food as well as his increasing ill health.[65]

The *second* factor is stress. In the early part of his life he had frequently to flee from persecution and for some time had to use assumed names to avoid detection and arrest. His great desire was to live the tranquil life of a scholar, but this was denied him when he was reluctantly drawn into the religious situation of Geneva by his friend William Farel in 1536, at the age of twenty-seven. Much against his own inclination he was thrust into leadership of the Reformation in French-speaking Switzerland. This was due no less to his scholarly and intellectual ability than it was to his gifts of pastoral and political leadership and organisation which are so evident in the progress of the Reformation in Geneva. But his position exposed him to physical, mental and spiritual stress which took its full toll of his health.

The *third* factor is the full and exhausting programme of study, preaching and teaching which he followed during much of his time in Geneva. Prior to 1549, he preached thrice weekly in the evenings and three times on Sundays. After 1549 he preached every weekday in each alternate week, and then twice on Sundays. He delivered weekly lectures in French to the Genevan pastors at their Friday meeting for Bible study, and lectured twice weekly in Latin to the students who were in training for the ministry and service of the Church. From the year 1549 a trained shorthand writer was employed by the congregation, and his record formed the basis of some of Calvin's later commentaries on books of the Bible, which were an important part of his literary output.[66]

The *fourth* factor is the almost incredible literary activity in which Calvin engaged, in addition to his preaching and teaching. His ministerial colleague Nicolas Colladon wrote that 'the multitude and quality alone of his writings is enough to astonish every one who looks at them, and even more those who read them'.[67] So far as his letters were concerned, Calvin insisted on replying personally and in his own handwriting to his numerous correspondents. He felt that they would be offended if he replied through a secretary.[68] But there came a time when this became too much and in February 1551 we find him writing to his close friend Henry Bullinger at Zürich:

> I am so much exhausted by constant writing and so greatly broken down by fatigue, that I frequently feel an almost positive aversion to writing a letter.[69]

The result was that towards the end of the year 1551, Calvin was finally persuaded to employ secretaries to whom he dictated his replies to letters and who also helped with the literary work associated with his preaching and teaching.[70]

A *fifth* factor is the lack of exercise in his later years. His main exercise appears to have been horse-riding, but as we shall see below, this became very difficult when he developed conditions which made this painful. He went for an occasional walk in the country or around the city of Geneva, usually accompanied by his wife, and sometimes played quoits in the garden with his friends. He found a minor form of exercise in his fondness for the game of *clef*, played on the table in his living room. This game appears to have been a variety of shovel-board or shuffle-board in which keys were used instead of coins or discs.

A *final* factor is his chronic insomnia. In 1538, when he was twenty-nine, he wrote to Farel and spoke of 'the want of sleep, to which custom has so inured me' and than which 'there is nothing more destructive of my health'.[71] The first statement is ambiguous. It may mean that his custom has been to go without sleep in order to do more work, or it may mean that he has become accustomed to not sleeping due to other causes not under the control of his will. Whichever is the meaning, it is clear that Calvin realises that his insomnia is detrimental to his health.

Other general symptoms which Calvin describes in his letters are those of headache, dyspepsia and fever which lead us on to a discussion of the various systemic disorders from which he suffered during his life. These we shall discuss under the different systems of the body which were affected by them. However, before we do so, it is appropriate to take a brief look at Calvin's psychiatric history.

Psychiatric History

The question here is whether Calvin suffered from any psychiatric disorder during his life. Several suggestions of what he might have suffered from have been made.

Stress-related syndromes

We have already described stress as one of the factors which affected Calvin's health and as we discuss the symptoms of the systemic disorders which Calvin suffered from, we shall find several which may be related to stress rather than to organic disease. These include headache which may be manifested as classical migraine, and attacks of abdominal pain.

Anxiety

Exposure to stress may also produce anxiety and there are many situations described in Calvin's letters about which Calvin must have been very anxious. These include times when his own life was threatened and the lives of his colleagues and fellow-believers.

A recent biographer of the Reformer has claimed that 'Calvin was a singularly anxious man and, as a reformer, fearful and troubled' and that 'his anxiety drove him through his career of strenuous and distinguished accomplishment'.[72] This claim and its relevance to Calvin's mental health, depends on what we understand by the term 'anxiety'. If by anxiety we mean an intense concern or fervent desire that something will happen, then there is no doubt that Calvin was an anxious man. He was intensely concerned about the progress of the gospel and the upbuilding of the Church in both France and Switzerland. It is impossible to read his letters without becoming conscious of these concerns of his. In this sense, we may agree that his anxiety was manifest throughout his career.

Anxiety may also be described as a feeling of apprehension or fear in the face of an immediate life-threatening situation. Calvin describes a situation of this kind in his farewell address to the ministers of Geneva, when he reminded them of how hostile persons had fired forty or fifty arquebus shots at his house one evening. He admitted that he had been very frightened on that occasion.[73]

In both these cases, Calvin's anxiety was a normal response to the cares of official and personal responsibility and to incidents of personal danger. We have no evidence that his anxiety was pathological, the symptom of an underlying emotional mental disorder.

Compulsive neurosis

An attempt at a specific psychiatric diagnosis in Calvin's case was made by Oskar Pfister, a Swiss Freudian analyst. This author regarded Calvin as 'the pitiable victim of a compulsive neurosis that compelled him to reshape the message of Jesus and the Apostles, producing a harsh substitute for the Gospel, and drove him to acts of cruelty'.[74] However, in order to reach this diagnosis, Pfister had to ignore so much of what is known about Calvin that, to quote McNeill, 'the reader familiar with the Reformer's work as a whole finds Pfister describing a man who was not there'.[75]

It will be noted that the manifestations of the psychiatric disorders from which Calvin is alleged to have suffered may all be normal psychological responses to life-affecting situations, namely, stress, anxiety and compulsion. None of them became permanent features of his personality, though each may have been temporarily manifested by him on occasions.

Systemic Disorders

We now turn to consider the systemic disorders and diseases from which Calvin appears to have suffered during his life.

The nervous system

Headache is the main symptom referable to this system. In some letters he speaks simply of 'a severe headache' which makes writing difficult and even confines him to bed for several days. More specifically he speaks of 'my migraine' and tells one correspondent that this is 'a complaint to which I am but too subject'.[76] In a letter to Farel he mentions that he had taken some pills for a headache which presumably were sedative as well as analgesic, for they prevented him from leaving the house to visit Farel's sick nephew.[77]

He began to have attacks of migraine while he was still a student at the Collège de Montaigu.[78] In one letter he speaks of an attack of migraine which was so severe that it was very painful to open his mouth, a feature which might be a more appropriate description of trigeminal neuralgia (*tic douloureux*).[79] His treatment for this complaint of migraine was to starve himself of food for one or two days for he believed that starvation was its only cure.[80] It is interesting that he does not mention headache or migraine in his letter to the physicians at Montpellier in 1564. This may mean that it had ceased to trouble him by then, for modern experience is that the condition not uncommonly remits after the age of fifty years.

It might be appropriate to note here that Calvin never complained of toothache, so far as we can discover. Owen Chadwick mentions a story that it was in the time of Calvin that the first dentist came to practice in Geneva, but he was only allowed to do so after he had been interviewed by Calvin to establish his reputability.[81]

The alimentary system

The weakness of his stomach or abdomen (*imbecillitas ventriculi*) of which Beza spoke in his Latin biography, manifested itself in different ways.[82] He was liable to have attacks of acute indigestion especially if he ate too big a meal.[83] He describes this familiarly as 'my dyspepsia' (*mea cruditas*) and usually treats it by rigid fasting.[84]

He suffered from attacks of abdominal pain of a griping or colicky nature (*tormina ventriculi*) which could be very severe.[85] He had chronic constipation for which Beza tells us that he took aloes, a stimulant purgative, to 'an immoderate degree'.[86] In modern practice, the use of aloes would not be recommended in a patient who also suffered from haemorrhoids since it does not soften the stool sufficiently. The combination of attacks of abdominal pain and constipation would suggest that Calvin suffered from what is today called 'the irritable bowel syndrome', which is recognised as occurring in conscientious subjects working under stress such as Calvin was and did.

There are several references in his letters to attacks of dysentery by which is meant infective diarrhoea. Such attacks must have been not uncommon in his time due to the lack of understanding of the need for good food hygiene and the means by which it could be achieved.[87]

He was afflicted with roundworms (*ascarides*) and describes the local irritation caused by their presence and movement in the rectum and anal area prior to their migration out of the anus or their expulsion in the faeces. By the time he wrote his letter to the physicians at Montpellier he had found relief from this condition.[88]

Finally under the alimentary system we must mention the haemorrhoids from which Calvin suffered. At first, he describes them as blind haemorrhoids (*haemorrhoidae caecae*) 'from which it is not possible to force blood', which presumably means that they did not bleed but could be seen as they prolapsed.[89] Later they did bleed and became ulcerated, and this made horse-riding very uncomfortable and even impossible for him.[90] Beza tells us that during the last five years of Calvin's life he occasionally lost considerable quantities of blood from his haemorrhoids.[91] The anaemia produced by this loss of blood in this way would increase his physical weakness.

Two of his modern biographers speak of an anal stricture which they say was produced by his haemorrhoids.[92] There is no evidence for this condition, and also an anal or rectal stricture is not recognised as a complication of haemorrhoids.

The respiratory system

A number of his letters refer to the upper respiratory tract infections which attacked Calvin from time to time. In a letter written soon after he first arrived in Geneva in 1536 he speaks of being attacked by a violent catarrh (*vehementi catarrho*) which settled on his upper gum (*in superiorum gingivam*) and lasted at least ten days in spite of his being bled twice, having several fomentations applied and taking double doses of medicine.[93] This presumably was some form of inflammation of the gum perhaps secondary to an acute maxillary sinusitis. Four years later he speaks of catarrh and the stuffing of the head, as 'a malady so frequent with me that it gave me no concern'.[94] However, the catarrh produced headaches and sometimes the infection spread down the respiratory tract to produce hoarseness and coughing. There are a number of references to coughing which is sometimes so severe that he has to stop writing.[95]

On three occasions (in 1558, 1561 and 1564) he complained of pain in the side of his chest. This pain was so severe that it kept him from writing,[96] and on one occasion lasted at least six weeks so that he had to cease all active work.[97] Calvin describes this pain as *dolor lateris* which is the term Latin medical authors commonly use to denote the pain of pleurisy.[98]

In his letter to the physicians of Montpellier, Calvin mentions coughing up blood.[99] The first time this occurred was in December 1559. On Sunday the 24th he was preaching to a crowded congregation in St Peter's Church in Geneva when he was forced to stop by a violent fit of coughing. This recurred during the following evening, when he coughed up much blood.[100] He had a further haemoptysis in February 1560 when he nearly choked on a large clot of blood which he coughed up from his lungs.[101] In October of that same year he writes of yet another haemoptysis.[102] In his biography of Calvin, Colladon records that over the next few years Calvin had two or three more episodes of haemoptysis.[103]

In the month before his death, in a letter to Bullinger, Calvin speaks of his lungs being so full of 'phlegmatic humours that my respiration is difficult and interrupted', and of how his cough and difficulty in breathing leave him no voice to continue dictating the letter.[104] Also Beza, describing the preaching of his last sermon on 6 February 1564, notes the breathlessness (*asthma*) of Calvin's delivery at that time.[105] In his farewell address to the ministers of Geneva on 28 April 1564, Calvin himself speaks of 'this shortness of breath which oppresses me more and more'.[106] In view of these symptoms it is not surprising to find Beza suggesting that he suffered from pulmonary tuberculosis (*phthisis*).[107]

The urinary system

Also in his letter to the physicians of Montpellier, Calvin describes how in the summer of the previous year (1563), he had an attack of 'nephritis'.[108] By this term he means simply a disease of the kidneys, for the term nephritis was derived from the Greek term *nosos nephritis* (disease of the kidneys) and did not at first have the more precise pathological meaning which it has today.[109] It is clear from his description that the kidney disease from which he suffered was renal calculus or stone.

In a letter to Margaret, Queen of Navarre, dated June 1st 1563, he gives a classic description of the attacks of renal colic caused by the passage of a renal calculus down the ureter, which he began to experience in the previous month.[110] The pain which this condition causes is one of the most severe known to medicine and fully justifies the adjectives used by Calvin when he describes it as 'very acute', 'extraordinary', 'desperate', 'exquisite' and 'excruciating'. When the pain came on, it numbed his senses and made thought impossible. A month later he writes to Bullinger in Zurich and gives more details of these attacks. He tells his friend that after several weeks, the pain became less as the stone found its way down the ureter into the bladder. Once it reached the bladder, it produced urinary retention and his doctor suggested that he should go for a ride on a horse to see if the jolting this produced, would result in the passage of the stone through the urethra. When he returned from the horse-ride he passed blood mixed with foul-smelling urine (*sanguis faeculentus*). Next day he was able to pass a stone the size of a hazelnut but only after 'excruciating tortures (*acerbiores cruciatus)'*.[111] This was followed by a copious haematuria which was only controlled by the introduction of human milk through a syringe into the urethra.[112] Calvin tells the Montpellier physicians that since this initial episode he has passed many stones, and he has a feeling of heaviness around the region of his kidneys which suggests that there are still more stones there. This experience of Calvin's produced the comment from Doumergue that his kidneys were just like a quarry (*une carrière* or *lapidicina*).[113] Calvin's comment after he had passed the original larger stone was that 'it seems now that I begin to live anew for the last two days since I am delivered of these pains'.[114]

In April 1564, about six weeks before he died, Calvin writes to Bullinger to say that once again a stone had lodged in his bladder and was giving him exquisite pain. This time, treatment by horse-riding was out of the question for 'an ulcer in my abdomen' was giving him excruciating pain even when he sat or lay down. His doctors had tried a number of remedies but all to no avail.[115]

The locomotor system

The origin of these renal stones becomes obvious when we turn to consider the disease of the locomotor system from which Calvin suffered. He describes it as gout, and it is well known that one of the complications of gout is the formation of renal stones due to increased excretion of uric acid in the urine. This combination of arthritis and renal stone suggests that   Calvin suffered from classical gout.

He appears to have suffered from time to time from the acute form of gout which the ancient Greek physicians called *podagra* since it affected the foot. Beza uses this word to describe the acute attack of excruciating pain that Calvin had in his right foot at the end of his attack of quartan fever in 1559.[116] In a letter to Beza of October 1561, Calvin describes another attack of podagra also affecting his right foot and gives some indication of how it is being treated. A bed cradle is being used to keep the bedclothes off the foot and fomentations of oil are being applied to the painful area. He says that he finds the smell of the oil quite nauseating.[117] The attacks of gout affected his walking about and he tells the physicians of Montpellier in his letter to them of 8th February 1564, that this has condemned him latterly to a purely sedentary way of life.[118] Two years before this he wrote in a letter to Bullinger that 'God has put fetters on my feet (*Deus me compedibus ligatum tenet*)'.[119]

In the same letter to the physicians of Montpellier, Calvin describes how he began to have acute attacks of pain in the calves of his legs following an attack of quartan fever. These recurred several times and finally affected his ankle and knee joints, after which they appear to have ceased. He gives no date for the onset of these attacks, but they may be those which were associated with the prolonged episode of quartan fever which began in October, and which Beza ascribed to gout as we have just mentioned.

Febrile Diseases

In the sixteenth century, fever was still regarded as a disease rather than a symptom. The use of the clinical thermometer was still two centuries in the future. Even after its invention by Sanctorius of Padua (1561-1636) in the seventeenth century, it was hardly used until the end of the eighteenth.[120] It was said of Carl Wunderlich (1815-1877) of Württemburg who introduced the individual temperature chart into clinical use, that 'he found fever a disease and left it a symptom'.[121]

In the absence of a thermometer, the diagnosis of fever depended on the recognition of an increase in body heat by the patient or its detection by the hand of the physician laid on his skin. Small rises of body temperature would easily be overlooked by these methods.

The different types of fever which were recognised in sixteenth century Europe were those described centuries before by Plato[122] and Hippocrates[123] in Greek terms, and then by Celsus in Latin.[124] These were classified as follows:

I   Continuous fevers

These occur in the most severe, difficult and fatal of the acute diseases.

II   Intermittent fevers:

1   *Febris quotidiana* which occurred every day.

2   *Febris tertiana* which occurred every second day and of which two varieties were recognised:

(a) *Febris tertiana* with regular remission every second day.

(b) *Febris semitertiana* in which the fever did not entirely remit in the intervening day. This type was regarded as the most fatal of all the fevers.

3   *Febris quartana* which occurred at two-day intervals.

Fevers of this kind are the least fatal and least difficult, but are the longest of all.

III   Irregular fevers.

As we seek to understand and even identify the febrile diseases which may have been prevalent in the sixteenth century in Europe and have affected Calvin, it is important to bear in mind the warning of Creighton, writing of the same period. He wrote:

Not only the term 'ague', but also the terms 'intermittent', 'tertian', and more specially 'quartan', can hardly be taken in their modern sense as restricted to malarial or climatic fevers. An intermittent or paroxysmal character of fevers was made out on various grounds to suit the traditional Galenic or Greek teaching; but the paroxysms and intermissions were not associated specially with the rise and fall of body temperature.[125]

Nevertheless, we know that malaria was present in Europe in the sixteenth century, and that it is the disease *par excellence* which is characterised by periodicity.[126] It was known more specifically as 'marsh ague'. In Calvin's time much excavation was carried out in and around Geneva in order to improve the defences of the city, and Beza reported that there were many outbreaks of intermittent fever at that time. This may have been because of infected malarial mosquitoes which bred in the rain-filled pools left in the excavated areas.[127]

Calvin's febrile illnesses

There are occasional references in Calvin's letters to fever which is not further described and not related to any other symptoms. Conversely there are references to symptoms or diseases which would be expected to be accompanied by fever, but in which fever is not mentioned. However, there are three attacks of febrile illness which Calvin describes in some detail in his letters.

The first one we have already mentioned. It occurred when Calvin was at the end of his honeymoon in September 1540.[128]

It began with an upper respiratory tract infection characterised by nasal congestion, cough and hoarseness. After three days the cough ceased but in the evening of the third day he fainted and retired to bed. He then had a severe rigor accompanied by fever. The following evening he again fainted and had frequent rigors followed by fever and heavy sweating which soaked the mattress. Calvin then recognised it as a *febris tertiana* for it continued with shooting pains and rigors. However he does not say how long the attack lasted, but it left him very weak and unable to deal with his correspondence for some time. During this attack Calvin mentions that his wife also became feverish, but in her case she had frequent vomiting over a period of eight days before she recovered. This may mean that they had contracted the same infection. The nature of this infection may have been a benign tertian (vivax) malaria, but the prior upper respiratory tract infection may suggest that it was an acute bronchopneumonia in Calvin's case, perhaps complicated by malaria.

The second attack occurred in May 1556 as he was preaching in Geneva.[129] Its onset was so sudden and so severe that he had to leave the pulpit with his sermon unfinished. The attack lasted for at least six

weeks. It was described by Calvin as a *febris tertiana* but he gives no
clinical details about it.[130] He became so ill that he ceased to write and
dictate letters, and reports of his death began to circulate in France,
which led to a service of thanksgiving for his death by the canons of
the cathedral at Noyon, his native place.[131] However, the reports were
premature, for the attack ended in recovery.

'The long illness'

The third attack of fever began in October 1558 and lasted until the
following May. No wonder Calvin called it 'the long illness (*la longue
maladie*)'.[132] This time he described it as *febris quartana*, and said that
this was the first time that he had suffered from an attack of this kind
of fever; so much so, that he did not recognise its nature until he
experienced the fourth paroxysm.[133] On each occasion the paroxysm
began with shivering and an exacerbation of his usual aches and pains.
The symptoms which accompanied the fever during this illness were
increased physical weakness, loss of appetite, thirst, dyspepsia and
constipation.[134]

One specific physical sign which appears to have been noted by
Calvin's doctors at this time was enlargement of the spleen. According
to the humoral theory of bodily function which was still the main
basis of medical practice in the sixteenth century, the spleen was
regarded as the organ which received the unclean matter which
accumulated in the region of the liver during disease, especially disease
accompanied by fever. As a result of this accumulation of bile, the
spleen became enlarged.[135] Part of the treatment for diseases in which
the spleen was found to be enlarged was, therefore, to attempt to expel
these excess 'bilious humours (*humores melancholicos*)' from the
spleen. The fact that Calvin's doctors attempted to do this by massage
and exerting pressure on the abdomen must mean that they had
discovered that his spleen was enlarged.[136]

Calvin also records other details of the treatment he is receiving
from his doctors for his quartan fever. These shed some light on the
therapeutic practices of the sixteenth century and show that these
were not very different from those described by Celsus in the first
century AD.[137] He was kept in bed with a double skin coverlet over
him. He was put on a light diet of 'the best and most digestible kinds
of food', which he found insipid and even loathsome. He was given
undiluted Burgundy wine which did not really quench his thirst.
When he was allowed other types of wine, these were usually mixed
with bitters such as absinthe in order to stimulate his appetite. Fluids
appear to have been restricted, for Calvin admits that when he
becomes very thirsty he does drink more than his doctors allow him.
Otherwise, he was the ideal patient for he says that 'in everything I
take care not to deviate one hair's breadth from the doctors'

prescription'. He developed severe constipation for which his doctors prescribed enemas (*clysteres*) which Calvin said was 'a state very alien to my usual habits'. However, even after nearly six weeks of this treatment, Calvin writes to his German friend Melanchthon and can report little improvement in his condition.[138]

In his Latin biography of Calvin, Beza adds more detail about this disease of *febris quartana*.[139] He describes it as 'a disease which we have at length learned, by too sad experience, is justly regarded by medical men as fatal to those who are advanced in years'. It commonly lasted for a long time and Beza suggests that it was unusual for it to last only eight months as it did in Calvin's case. It normally resulted in complete physical exhaustion. Because of this, Calvin's doctors insisted that he stop preaching and lecturing, but they were not able to prevent him from dictating and writing letters. Indeed, we know that during this period he prepared the definitive edition of the *Institutes of the Christian Religion* in both Latin and French, and completed the second edition of his commentary on the book of the prophet Isaiah. He dedicated this latter work to Queen Elizabeth of England.

It was in a letter written in March 1559, towards the end of this period of illness, that Calvin mentions the first appearance of the blind haemorrhoids to which we have already referred. Presumably they were associated with the severe constipation for which he needed enemas. At the end of his illness he complained of sharp and severe pain in his legs,[140] and had the acute attack of gout which we mentioned above. When he resumed his duties he had to preach sitting down.[141]

There are several chronic febrile diseases which could fit the description of Calvin's serious illness of 1558-1559, but specific features are lacking in this description which might otherwise allow its precise identification. Walker suggested that the condition was 'severe nervous dyspepsia',[142] but we may safely dismiss this diagnosis for it does not even satisfy the initial criterion of the presence of fever. Other biographers have not made any attempt to identify the nature of this illness.

The nature of Calvin's febrile illnesses

Calvin suffered from both short-term and long-term fevers. His frequent references in his letters to attacks of catarrh suggest that one cause of his short-term fevers was infection of the upper respiratory tract. Another cause was probably influenza for we know that this disease was endemic in Europe in the sixteenth century. Twenty epidemics of this disease have been identified as occurring in Europe during that century, with notable ones in the years 1510, 1557 and 1580. That of 1580 was the world's first recorded pandemic.[143] A third cause of short-term attacks of fever would be malaria which we have already seen to be prevalent in Europe in the sixteenth century. Calvin would be exposed to infection with this disease in Geneva and also in the other areas of Europe to which he travelled.

The fact that his doctors discovered that his spleen was enlarged would appear to confirm the presence of malaria which could also explain his attacks of fever and shivering in the absence of effective specific antimalarial therapy. However, in the case of the long illness and the period of increased ill health which this illness initiated, ending finally in his death, symptoms appeared which cannot be explained on the basis of malaria alone. These symptoms could have been produced by pulmonary tuberculosis as Beza suggested soon after Calvin's death.[144] It has also been suggested that similar symptoms could result from the disease of the heart known as infective or bacterial endocarditis especially in its subacute form. The following table compares these three diseases in relation to the relevant symptoms described by Calvin.

Symptom	Chronic Malaria	Pulmonary Tuberculosis	Infective Endocarditis
Fever	Yes	Yes	Yes
Fatiguability	Yes	Yes	Yes
Emaciation	Yes	Yes	Yes
Anaemia	Yes	Yes	Yes
Cough	No	Yes	No
Haemoptysis	No	Yes	No *(unless in mitral stenosis)*
Pleuritic pain	No	Yes	No
Splenomegaly	Yes	No	Yes

This table confirms that it is unlikely that chronic malaria alone would explain all the symptoms of the long illness and its sequel. Its presence along with other diseases would however exacerbate the general symptoms of which Calvin complained. The table does suggest that pulmonary tuberculosis is a strong possibility for the cause of Calvin's long illness and for what followed that illness. Subacute infective endocarditis is also a possible cause of Calvin's ill health in the last six years of his life, but this diagnosis has certain implications which must now be discussed.

Infective endocarditis is a disease in which bacteria attach themselves to and invade the valves of the heart, which are abnormal either because they are congenitally deformed or have been damaged by some previous disease process. Most valves which are affected by this disease have been damaged in the course of an attack of acute rheumatic fever. This means that if Calvin suffered from infective endocarditis when he was nearly fifty years old, he would have had an attack of rheumatic fever earlier in his life which left him with permanent damage to his heart valves. He would then have developed one of the forms of chronic rheumatic heart disease which might affect and later restrict his physical activity. Eventually bacterial infection of a damaged valve or valves would occur which would lead to increasing ill health and death. Unfortunately, we have no specific evidence that Calvin passed through these stages in his medical history because the significance of the signs which would indicate that he did so were not understood in the sixteenth century. The association of rheumatic fever with endocarditis was only recognised by Jean-Baptiste Bouillard of Angoulême in 1836,[145] although it is possible that acute rheumatic fever had been described by Hippocrates in the fifth century BC.[146] Our conclusion must be that infective endocarditis is a possible cause of Calvin's increased ill health in the last years of his life, but it is unlikely because specific evidence is lacking.

Calvin's Last Years

Whatever the nature of the long illness was, it was associated with a further and permanent deterioration in Calvin's health. From 1559 onwards, each remaining year of his life was marred by ill health and by the beginning of 1563 he was so weak that he was often carried to his duties in a chair or on horseback.[147] During the winter of that year his attendance at the weekly Consistory meeting became increasingly infrequent.

By February 1564 it was obvious that Calvin was seriously ill. On the morning of Wednesday 2 February, he preached on the First book of Kings in the Church of St Peter, and in the afternoon he gave his sixty-fifth lecture on the book of Ezekiel in the Academy which he had inaugurated in Geneva in 1559.[148] He was not well enough to preach or lecture for the remainder of that week, but on the Sunday in spite of obvious breathlessness, he gave his customary annual address to the General Council of Geneva.[149] Later the same day he preached on the Harmony of the gospels during the morning service in St Peter's. This proved to be his last sermon.

However, until the end of the month of March he still attended the regular meeting or *congrégation* of the ministers which was held for the study of the Bible each Friday morning at seven o'clock. At these meetings he would sometimes speak briefly and close with prayer.[150] On Easter Sunday, 2 April, he was taken by chair to the Church for the last time, when he received the sacrament of the Lord's Supper from the hands of his colleague Beza.

On 25 April, he made his will.[151] Soon after he had done this, Calvin asked if he might address the members of the Little Council in their Chamber in the City Hall, but they insisted that in view of his weakness they should come to him at his house. This they did on the 27th.[152] On the following day, the ministers of Geneva met at his house to hear his farewell address to them.[153] Finally, on 19 May he shared an evening meal at table with Beza and his colleagues and then retired to bed, never to rise from it again, although he still continued to dictate to his secretary.[154]

From that day and until his death, there was little change in his appearance. His whole body was so emaciated that nothing seemed left but his spirit. He remained conscious and perfectly sensible and intelligent, able to speak to his very last breath. He died very calmly and peacefully without any convulsion of his hands or feet, and not even with a deep sigh. When death came, according to his friend Beza, he looked much more like one sleeping than one dead.[155]

Cause of Death

Calvin died at 8pm as the sun was setting on Saturday 27 May 1564, 'whole and entire in sense and understanding' as the entry in the Register of the Council of Geneva described him.[156] He was fifty-four years of age and so had fulfilled his own estimate of the average expectation of life at that time. In a sermon on the Book of Job, preached when he was about forty-five, he had given this expectation as about fifty to sixty years.[157]

The question now arises of the cause of his death.

The factors which adversely affected his health from his student days to the end of his life have been mentioned above. These were his customary abstemiousness towards food, his strenuous involvement in public life, his prodigious literary activity, his lack of exercise and his chronic insomnia. To these may be added the effect of the anaemia produced by his attacks of malaria and the recurrent loss of blood from his haemorrhoids. None of these factors can be credited with causing his death, but they would combine to lower his resistance to disease and help to reduce him to what some of his friends described as 'a regular skeleton, a shadow rather than a substance', three months before he died.[158]

What then did cause his death? We may dismiss the suggestion that he died from chronic renal failure due to the obstructive effect of his renal stones on the urinary outflow.[159] In so far as decreased mental acuity is an early feature of chronic renal failure, it is unlikely that he suffered from this condition. He died in the full possession of his mental powers for 'he only stopped dictating about eight hours before he died, his voice at last playing him traitor'.[160] Also, Beza noted that his eyes 'sparkled to the moment of his death'.[161] These are not the features seen in one dying of chronic renal failure.

It is most probable that he died of infection. Some of his attacks of fever were probably malarial in origin, but it is unlikely that malarial infection was the primary cause of his death. It would however lower his resistance to disease still further and explain the enlargement of his spleen which was detected by his doctors.

A recent suggestion is that the immediate cause of Calvin's death was 'septic shock' due to septicaemia or blood-poisoning.[162] However, there is no evidence for this and it is quite unrelated to his previous medical history.

A more possible suggestion is that of subacute infective endocarditis as the cause of death. As we have already seen, this condition arises from a bacteraemia or invasion of the blood by bacteria which settle on heart valves previously damaged by rheumatic disease. If the long illness which Calvin had in 1558-1559 was subacute infective endocarditis, then it is possible that this was the eventual cause of his death although he survived that illness for another five years. Unfortunately, we have no information on the occurrence of this disease in the sixteenth century and its presence in Calvin's case is unlikely.

The most probable cause of Calvin's death is pulmonary tuberculosis. This accords with the contemporary opinion recorded by Beza, which was presumably the diagnosis of the doctors who attended Calvin.[163] The disease was present amongst the close associates of Calvin for it was recorded as the cause of the death of one of his personal secretaries some years later.[164] Also, the occurrence of frequent severe bouts of coughing and recurrent haemoptysis, together with pleuritic pain, breathlessness and audible physical signs in the chest ('lungs full of phlegm'[165]) make pulmonary tuberculosis the most likely cause of Calvin's death.

Burial

His body was buried at 2pm on Sunday 28 May 1564, wrapped in a linen shroud and encased in a plain wooden coffin 'in the common cemetery called Plein Palais' in Geneva, as he himself had requested.[166] His funeral was conducted without any special pomp or elaborate ceremony, in the presence of a great assembly of people from all walks of life from the city of Geneva and elsewhere. Also at his request, no gravestone was erected and so the site of his grave is today unknown. He wished to be buried like Moses, out of reach of idolatry.[167] In modern times, a stone measuring about a foot square has been placed in the cemetery inscribed with the initials 'J.C.' to remind visitors that John Calvin is buried there, even though the exact location of his grave is not known.[168]

NOTES AND REFERENCES
FOR CHAPTER 2

Key to abbreviations

OC = G.Baum, E.Cunitz & E.Reuss (eds), *Ioannis Calvini Opera quae supersunt omnia* (Brunswick: Schwelschke, 1863-1900), 59 vols. Calvin's letters are in vols. 10 to 20 and the contemporary biographies of Calvin are in vol. 21. In the present chapter, Beza's Latin biography is quoted as 'Beza OC' (called Beza 2 by Parker 186), and Colladon's French biography as 'Colladon OC'.

ET = J.Bonnet (ed), *Letters of John Calvin in Latin & French*. English translation by D.Constable & M.R.Gilchrist (New York: Burt Franklin, 1972). Reprint of 1858 edition, 4 vols. 'The English translation of Bonnet's collection of the letters is useless for serious study, abounding as it does in gross errors of translation and mistakes in dating' (Parker 186).

Beza ET = T.Beza, *The Life of John Calvin*. English translation by Henry Beveridge of the Latin *Vita Calvini*. In *Tracts relating to the Reformation* (Edinburgh: Calvin Translation Society, 1844), **1**:xix-c.

HCR = A.L.Herminjard, *Correspondance des Reformateurs dans les pays de langue française recueillie et publiée, 1512-1544* (Geneva: H Georg et Cie, 1866-1897), 9 vols. Herminjard is chiefly responsible for the dating of Calvin's letters which is now generally accepted and is the one mainly followed by the editors of OC (Parker 186-187).

Key to authors and sources quoted

Bouwsma = W.J.Bouwsma, *John Calvin: A Sixteenth Century Portrait* (New York: Oxford University Press, 1988).

Cadier = J.Cadier, 'Les maladies de Calvin et ses relations avec les médecins montpelliérains' in *Monspel. Hippocra.* (1958) 1(2):6-12. Cadier was Doyen de la Faculté de théologie de Montpellier et Président de la Société Calviniste de France.

Cooke = C.L.Cooke, 'Calvin's Illnesses and their relation to Christian Vocation' in T.George (ed), *John Calvin and the Church* (Louisville: Westminster/John Knox Press, 1990), 59-70.

Doumergue = E.Doumergue, *Jean Calvin: Les hommes et les choses de son temps* (Lausanne: Georges Bridel et Cie, 1899-1927), 7 vols.

Doumergue, Caractère = E.Doumergue, Le Caractère de Calvin (Neuilly: La Cause, 1931).

Ganoczy = A.Ganoczy, *The Young Calvin* (Edinburgh: T & T Clark, 1987).

Greef = W.de Greef, *The Writings of John Calvin* (Grand Rapids: Baker Book House, 1993).

Hunt = R.N.C.Hunt, *Calvin* (London: The Centenary Press, 1933).

Lefranc = A.Lefranc, *La Jeunesse de Calvin* (Paris: Librairie Fischbacher, 1888).

McGrath = A.E.McGrath, *A Life of John Calvin: A Study in the Shaping of Western Culture* (Oxford: Basil Blackwell, 1990).

McNeill = J.T.McNeill, *The History and Character of Calvinism* (New York: Oxford University Press, 1954).

Montpellier = OC 20:252-254/ET 4:358-360 (Letter of Calvin to the Physicians of the Faculty of Medicine of the University of Montpellier in France, 8 Feb. 1564).

Parker = T.H.L.Parker, *John Calvin* (London: JM Dent, 1982).

Penning = L.Penning, *The Life and Times of Calvin* (London: Kegan Paul, Trench & Trübner, 1912).

Potter & Greengross = G.R.Potter & M.Greengross, *John Calvin* (London: Edwin Arnold, 1983).

Reyburn = H.Y.Reyburn, *John Calvin: His Life, Letters & Work* (London: Hodder & Stoughton, 1914).

Schaff = P.Schaff, *History of the Christian Church: The Swiss Reformation* (Edinburgh: T & T Clark, 1893), 2 vols.

Walker = W.Walker, *John Calvin: The Organiser of Reformed Protestantism (1509-1564)* (New York: G.P.Putnam, 1906).

Wendel = F.Wendel, *Calvin: The Origins & Development of His Religious Thought* (London: Collins, 1963).

[1] Recent biographies of Calvin describe his medical history in only one or two sentences. See, for example, Bouwsma 30-31 and McGrath 195.

[2] Parker 4.

[3] Wendel 15.

[4] Montpellier OC 20:252 = ET 4.358. Dr Philibert Sarrazin, whom Calvin mentions in this letter, had succeeded Dr Benedict Textor as Calvin's physician after Textor died about 1556. Sarrazin was regarded as an excellent physician whose reputation extended far beyond Geneva. See Cadier 10 and Doumergue 3:511-512. The physicians of Montpellier in 1564 were Guillaume Rondolet, Antoine Saporta and Nicolas Dortoman, all Protestants. See Cadier 11.

[5] In 1532 Calvin latinised his family name to Calvinus when he published his first book, a Latin commentary on Seneca's *De Clementia* (On Mercy). This name became Calvin in French and English. The name Cauvin is derived from the word 'chauve', bald (So Doumergue, Caractère 18).

[6] See the genealogical table in P.Henry, *Das Leben Johann Calvins des grossen Reformators* (Hamburg: 1835-1844), 3, *Beilage* **16**:174. This table is omitted from the English translation by Henry Stebbing, *The Life & Times of John Calvin* (London: Whitaker, 1849). Colladon OC, **21**:53 speaks of Calvin as having four brothers, but Doumergue regards this as a mistake (Doumergue **1**:22, note 2).

[7] Lefranc 6.

[8] Lefranc (*Ibidem*) suggests there may be an indirect reference to Calvin's mother in his French treatise *Traicté des Reliques* (1543). In this Calvin describes a boyhood visit ('long ago') to the shrine of St Anne, mother of the Virgin Mary, at the Cistercian Abbaye d'Ourscamps, near Noyon, when he remembered kissing the relic of St Anne displayed there. According to a Noyon tradition, as one expression of her deep devotion, Calvin's mother was in the habit of visiting local shrines on appropriate feast days accompanied by her son John. The incident recalled by Calvin may thus have occurred on one of these visits with his mother and so provide an indirect reference to her. See OC **6**:422 and the English translation, 'Advantages from an Inventory of Relics' in *Tracts relating to the Reformation* (Edinburgh: Calvin Translation Society, 1844), **1**:329. Cp Doumergue **1**:42.

[9] His name first appears in a legal document dated 20th September 1481, according to Lefranc 2. Beza describes him as 'a person of no small judgement and prudence' (Beza OC **21**:121 = Beza ET xxi).

[10] Lefranc 5. Beza speaks of Calvin's parents as 'persons of good repute and in easy circumstances' (Beza OC **21**:121 = Beza ET xxi). Cp OC **21**:29.

[11] Lefranc 16-17 & 195-197; HCR **2**:394.

[12] Walker 46; Granoczy 71.

[13] Walker 56-57; Doumergue **1**:22-25.

[14] Walker 21.

[15] OC **13**:526 (Calvin to Cordier, 20 March 1550). Cp Lefranc 59.

[16] Colladon OC **21**:54. McGrath has produced evidence which suggests Calvin did not, in fact, attend the Collège de la Marche (See McGrath 22-24).

[17] Reyburn 10.

[18] McGrath 27-31.

[19] D.Erasmus, *Colloquies: Ichthyophagia* (A Fish Diet). English translation by C.R.Thompson (Chicago: Chicago University Press, 1965, 351-352). Erasmus was a man of mature age when he entered the Collège de Montaigu for he was already then in priestly orders and an established scholar. See F.M.Nichols, *The Epistles of Erasmus* (London: Longmans, Green & Co., 1901), 104.

[20] F.Rabelais, *Gargantua and Pantagruel* **1**:37 & **4**:22. Rabelais had never attended the Collège de Montaigu and probably only knew of conditions there from his reading of Erasmus. So Nichols FM. op. cit. 109. Cp Lefranc 64-65.

[21] McNeill 98. Cordier's Latin *Colloquies* were used in Latin lessons in the old parish schools of Scotland as examples of good Latin prose. (See C.G.McCrie (ed), *Beza's Icones: Contemporary Portraits of Reformers of Religion and Letters* (London: Religious Tract Society, 1909), 139.

[22] Beza OC **21**:121 = Beza ET xxi. Cp McNeill 100.

[23] Wendel 19.

[24] Ganoczy 49-55; McGrath 47-50.

[25] Beza OC **21**:121 = Beza ET xxii; Colladon OC **21**:54. See also Calvin in OC **31**:22 (French Preface to Commentary on the Book of Psalms) and Wendel 21.

[26] Colladon OC **21**:55. 'Il n'y a point de doute que telles veilles ne lui ayent bien offense sa santé.'

27 Beza OC **21**:122 = Beza ET xxiii.
28 Lefranc 75; Hunt 33.
29 McNeill 109.
30 McGrath 60.
31 Penning 80.
32 For accounts of his 'sudden conversion (*subita conversio*)' to the Reformed Faith see McGrath 69-73 and Parker 192-196. It has been suggested that the passage of Scripture which more than any other, influenced Calvin at the time of his conversion was Romans **1**:18-25, particularly verse 21. See F.L.Battles, *The Piety of John Calvin* (Grand Rapids: Baker Book House, 1978), 16.
33 Beza OC **21**:169 = Beza ET xcvii.
34 OC **10**:37 = HCR **3**:156 = ET **1**:41 (Calvin to Daniel, early 1534).
35 Doumergue **3**:500-501.
36 HCR **5**:230-231 note 19; Hunt 95.
37 OC **10**:332 = HCR **5**:267 = ET **1**:131 (Calvin to Farel, end March 1539).
38 OC **10**:340 = HCR **5**:291 = ET **1**:136 (Calvin to Farel, end April 1539).
39 Hunt 96.
40 Beza OC **21**:162-164 = Beza ET lxxxv-lxxxix = ET **4**:365-369 (Last Will and Testament of Master John Calvin). When Calvin died his whole effects, including all his books, were sold and realised less than 300 gold crowns or *écus* (Beza OC **21**:170 = Beza ET xcix).
41 Beza OC **21**:130 = Beza ET xxxvi. 'If the portraits we have of her are authentic, she was as elegant and sensitive a woman as the aristocratic tastes of the reformer would have required' (Wendel 66).
42 OC **13**:230-231 = ET **2**:216-217 (Calvin to Viret, 7 April 1549). In a letter written to Farel in May 1539, Calvin had described the kind of wife he sought; amongst his requirements was one that she should be concerned about his health. See OC **10**:348 = HCR **5**:314 = ET **1**:141 (Calvin to Farel, 19 May 1539).
43 OC **11**:83 = HCR **6**:312 = ET **1**:204-205 (Calvin to Farel, October 1540).
44 OC **12**:420 = HCR **8**:82-82 = ET **1**:335 (Calvin to Viret, 30 July 1542).
45 OC **12**:580-581 = ET **2**:138 (Calvin to Farel, 21 August 1547).
46 Dr Benedict Textor appears to have been a good physician but a difficult character (So Doumergue **3**:510-511). As their family physician, he charged the Calvins no fees and in gratitude, Calvin dedicated his commentary on Second Thessalonians to him in 1550 (OC **52**:181). See also Cadier 9-10; Greef 98.
47 OC **11**:430 = HCR **8**:109 = ET **1**:344 (Calvin to Viret, 19 August 1542).
48 See, for example, Jules Bonnet in ET **1**:420, note 2 and ET **2**:47, note 2.
49 OC **9**:576 = ET **1**:344, note 3 (Answer to the reproaches of Baudouin, 1561). In this response to François Baudouin, Calvin said that whilst it was true that he was now physically childless, he had spiritual children over the whole of Christendom ('*Atqui mihi filiorum sunt myriades in toto orbe Christiano*'). See also Doumergue **2**:471-472.
50 Colladon OC **21**:62.
51 Hunt 101; Penning 147.

[52]   OC **12**:202 = ET **2**:26 (Calvin to de Falais, 26 October 1545).

[53]   OC **13**:36 = ET **2**:176 (Calvin to Farel, 27 August 1548)

[54]   OC **13**:230 = ET **2**:216 (Calvin to Viret, 7 April 1549) and OC **13**:228-229 = ET **2**:217-219 (Calvin to Farel, 11 April 1549).

[55]   OC **53**:254 (Sermon No.2 on First Timothy). See also Parker 121.

[56]   OC **10**:37 = HCR **3**:156 = ET **1**:41 (Calvin to Daniel, early 1534).

[57]   Colladon OC **21**:56.

[58]   McGrath 16-17. In his biography of Calvin (1577), Bolsec suggested that Calvin died of some shameful sexual disease and this unsubstantiated calumny was repeated by Ernest Renault in 1899 when he wrote in an anti-Protestant pamphlet, 'Calvin mourut de la syphilis tout simplement'. See Cadier 11.

[59]   OC **9**:892 = ET **4**:374 (Calvin's farewell to the Geneva ministers, 28 April 1564).

[60]   OC **17**:14 = ET **4**:41 (Calvin to Hotman, 27 May 1559). While it is true that Beza describes Calvin as being 'naturally of a keen temper', but able to control it (Beza OC **21**:170 = Beza ET xcviii-xcix), it must be remembered that most descriptions of Calvin's temper come from his own letters or speeches, as in the quotations collected by Doumergue (See Doumergue, Caractère 16-17). Self-assessment of this kind readily leads to overstatement, especially in a person so spiritually sensitive as Calvin.

[61]   McGrath 17.

[62]   Schaff **2**.417.

[63]   Beza OC **21**:160 = Beza ET lxxxiii.

[64]   Colladon OC **21**:109.

[65]   Cooke 59-60. For the portraits of Calvin see E.Doumergue, *Iconographie Calvinienne* (Lausanne: Georges Bridel et Cie, 1909).

[66]   Colladon OC **21**:70-71. Cp Potter & Greengross 118. The first commentary which Calvin published was on the Epistle to the Romans, which appeared in Strasburg in March 1540 (Greef 94).

[67]   Colladon OC **21**:107. 'The literary activity of Calvin, whether we look at the number of or at the importance of his works, is not surpassed by any ecclesiastical writer, ancient or modern'(Schaff **1**:267). Cp Potter & Greengross 169.

[68]   OC **20**:131 (Jonvilliers to Bullinger, August 1563).

[69]   OC **12**:51 = ET **2**:304 (Calvin to Bullinger, 17 February 1551). Not only was Calvin exhausted by letter writing, he complains to one of his correspondents how he was often interrupted twenty or more times during the writing of a letter, thus breaking his train of thought. See OC **12**:330 = ET **2**:43 (Calvin to de Falais, April 1546).

[70]   Reyburn 277-280.

[71]   OC **10**:273 = HCR **5**:166 = ET **1**:100 (Calvin to Farel, 24 October 1538).

[72]   Bouwsma 32.

[73]   OC **9**:892 = ET **4**:374.

[74]   O.R.Pfister, *Calvinus Eingreifen in die Hexen und Hexenprozesse von Peney, 1545* (Zurich: 1947). This proposed diagnosis is based on an examination of the involvement of Calvin in the witch trials at Peney in 1545.

[75]   McNeill 230.

[76] OC **14**:474 = ET **4**:412 (Calvin to Blaurer, 14 February 1552).

[77] OC **10**:237 = ET **1**:78 (Calvin to Farel, 20 August 1538).

[78] J.Cadier, *The Man God Mastered* (London: Inter-Varsity Press, 1960), 22, quoting Florimond de Raemond, *Histoire de l'Hérésie de ce Siècle* (Paris, 1623), **VII**:10,885.

[79] OC **12**:392 = ET **2**:74 (Calvin to de Falais, 4 October 1546).

[80] Beza OC **21**:160 = Beza ET lxxxiii. On one occasion he starved himself for three days before the attack of migraine abated. See OC **13**:451 (Calvin to Farel, 18 November 1549).

[81] O.Chadwick, *The Reformation* (Harmondsworth: Penguin Books, 1964), 86. This story may be apocryphal.

[82] Beza OC **21**:122 = Beza ET xxiii.

[83] OC **11**:83 = HCR **6**:312 = ET **1**:205 (Calvin to Farel, October 1540).

[84] OC **17**:384 = ET **3**:482 (Calvin to Melanchthon, 19 November 1558).

[85] OC **12**:26 = ET **2**:176 (Calvin to Farel, 27 August 1548).

[86] Beza OC **21**:160 = Beza ET lxxxiii. Beza attributes the appearance of haemorrhoids in Calvin's case to 'the immoderate use of aloes' which Calvin presumably took for the treatment of constipation.

[87] OC **10**:277 = HCR **5**:140 = ET **1**:90 (Calvin to Farel, 15 October 1538); OC **16**:332 = ET **3**:302 (Calvin to Bullinger, 29 November 1556) and ET **4**:381 (Calvin to Daniel, June/July 1534).

[88] Montpellier OC **20**:253 = ET **4**:359.

[89] OC **17**:468 = ET **4**:31 (Calvin to Vermilius alias Peter Martyr, 2 March 1559).

[90] Montpellier OC **20**:253 = ET **4**:359.

[91] Beza OC **21**:160 = Beza ET lxxxiii.

[92] Reyburn 321; Cooke 70, note 13. The suggestion of the presence of an anal or rectal stricture in Calvin's case appears to have arisen because of a sentence in his letter to the physicians of Montpellier in which he speaks of his haemorrhoids being 'so swollen that, because of the constriction whatever I force out is rather like a hen's droppings (*venae sunt turgidae ut quod egero intus ipsa constrictione tematum parum a gallinae excrementis differat*)'. This sentence should probably be understood to describe the possible obstructive effect of the swollen haemorrhoids rather than an actual stricture as understood surgically. However, this sentence is probably not authentic and the editors of the text add a footnote saying, 'The text seems to be corrupt (*Textus corruptus videtur*)'. See Montpellier OC **20**:254, note 11.

[93] OC **10**:63 = HCR **4**:36 = ET **1**:45 (Calvin to Daniel, 13 October 1536).

[94] OC **11**:83 = HCR **6**:312 = ET **1**:204 (Calvin to Farel, end September 1540)

[95] OC **10**:396 = HCR **6**:52 = ET **1**:156 (Calvin to Farel, 8 October 1539).

[96] OC **18**:466 = ET **4**:189 (Calvin to Bullinger, 24 May 1561).

[97] OC **17**:95 = ET **4**:429 (Calvin to Macarius, 16 March 1558).

[98] See, e.g. Celsus, *De Medicina* **4**:13,1 (Loeb edition **1**:405). The word *latus* means 'the side of the upper part of the trunk in human beings', and in particular is used to denote 'the side of the chest (esp. as affected by pleurisy)'. See *Oxford Latin Dictionary* (Oxford: Clarendon Press, 1982), 1008, s.v. 'latus'.

[99] Montpellier OC **20**:253 = ET **4**:358

100 OC **21**:725; OC **18**:3 (Beza to Bullinger, 1 January 1560).

101 OC **18**:14 (Calvin to Blaurer, February 1560).

102 OC **18**:214 = ET **4**:141 (Calvin to Gallars, 3 October 1560).

103 Colladon OC **21**:89.

104 OC **20**:283 = ET **4**:363 (Calvin to Bullinger, 6 April 564).

105 Beza OC **21**:160 = Beza ET lxxxii. See also Calvin's last letter to Farel: OC **20**:302-303 = ET **4**:364 (Calvin to Farel, 2 May 1564).

106 OC **9**:982 = ET **4**:373 (Calvin's Farewell to the Geneva Ministers, 28 Apr. 1564).

107 Beza OC **21**:160 = Beza ET lxxxiii. See also OC **20**:39 (Beza to Blaurer, 6 June 1563).

108 Montpellier OC **20**:254 = ET **4**:359.

109 *Oxford English Dictionary* (Oxford: Clarendon Press, 1971), compact edition **1**:1913, s.v. 'Nephritis'.

110 OC **20**:34 = ET **4**:318 (Calvin to Margaret, Queen of Navarre, 1 June 1563). See also OC **20**:36 (Jonvilliers to Bullinger, 9 June 1563).

111 OC **20**:54 = ET **4**:321 (Calvin to Bullinger, 2 July 1563).

112 Montpellier OC **20**:254 = ET **4**:359.

113 Doumergue **3**:524.

114 OC **20**:34 = ET **4**:318 (Calvin to the Queen of Navarre, 1 June 1563).

115 OC **20**:283 = ET **4**:362 (Calvin to Bullinger, 6 April 1564). Calvin's reference to 'an ulcer in my abdomen' is not clear. It probably refers to his ulcerated haemorrhoids since it produced pain on sitting or lying, and particularly when riding.

116 Beza OC **21**:160 = Beza ET lxxxi.

117 OC **19**:30 (Calvin to Beza, 7 October 1561).

118 Montpellier OC **20**:254 = ET **4**:359.

119 OC **19**:602 = ET **4**:285 (Calvin to Bullinger, 27 December 1562).

120 D.Guthrie, *A History of Medicine* (London: Thomas Nelson, 1945), 257. See also I.Blumenthal, 'The Development of the Clinical Thermometer' in *Proceedings of the Royal College of Physicians of Edinburgh* (1988) **28**: 67-72.

121 F.H.Garrison, *Introduction to the History of Medicine.* (Philadelphia: Saunders, 1929), 431. In 1868 Wunderlich published his classic work *Das Verhalten der Eigenwärme in Krankheiten* (The Temperature in Disease) which Garrison (op.cit., 430) described as 'the very foundation of our present clinical thermometry'. This work was based on observations made on nearly 25,000 patients.

122 Plato, *Timaeus* 86A (Loeb edition 233). Plato traces the different types of fever to excesses of the Four Elements of Empedocles in the body. Continued fever is due to an excess of fire; quotidian fever to an excess of air; tertian fever to an excess of water and quartan fever to an excess of earth .

123 Hippocrates, *On the Nature of Man* 15:1-40 (Loeb edition **4**:39-41). According to Hippocrates, fever comes from bile and the different types of fever are due to the presence of different amounts of bile in the body. The presence of an abnormally large amount produces continued fever and of the least abnormal amount produces quartan fever. In another of his writings, Hippocrates gives an even more detailed list of the types of fever. See his *Epidemics* **1**:5 & 24 (Loeb edition **1**:155 & 181-185).

[124] Celsus, *De Medicina* **3**:3 (Loeb edition **1**:227).

[125] C.Creighton, *A History of Epidemics in Britain* (Cambridge: Cambridge University Press, 1894), **1**:411.

[126] L.A.Bruce Chwatt & J. de Zulueta, *The Rise and Fall of Malaria in Europe: A Historico-epidemiological Study* (Oxford: Oxford University Press, 1980).

[127] Ch.Joyeux, 'Le Paludisme - Extension et Régression' in *Bull Soc neuchâtel Sci nat* (1942) **67**:1-96.

[128] OC **11**:83 = HCR **6**:312 = ET **1**:204-205 (Calvin to Farel, October 1540).

[129] Beza OC **21**:152 = Beza ET lxx.

[130] OC **16**:218 = ET **3**:284 (Calvin to Bullinger, 1 July 1556).

[131] Beza OC 21:152 = Beza ET lxx.

[132] OC **17**:440 = ET **4**:21 (Calvin to the French Church at Strasbourg, 23 Feb. 1559).

[133] OC **17**:361 = ET **3**:477 (Calvin to Toussain, 12 October 1558). But he also calls it *febris tertiana* in OC **17**:14 = ET **4**:41 (Calvin to Hotman, 27 May 1559).

[134] OC **17**:384 = ET **3**:482 (Calvin to Melanchthon, 19 November 1558).

[135] Plato, *Timaeus* 72C (Loeb edition 189). The ancient Greek physicians had already noted the association of enlargement of the spleen with marshy places in summer. See Hippocrates, *Airs, Waters & Places* **7**:6-20 (Loeb edition **1**:85) and Aretaeus, *Chronic Diseases* **1**:14. This can be explained today in terms of the natural history of malaria, but the reason for the association was not known in ancient times.

[136] OC **17**:384 = ET **3**:482 (Calvin to Melanchthon, 19 November 1558).

[137] Celsus, *De Medicina* 4:16 (Loeb edition **1**:415-419).

[138] OC **17**:384 = ET **3**:482 (Calvin to Melanchthon, 19 November 1558). Cp Reyburn 321-322. Calvin had a high opinion of physicians and their responsibilities. This can be seen from the care he took before recommending an individual physician. See ET **4**:381 (Calvin to Daniel, June/July 1534).

[139] Beza OC **21**:156 = Beza ET lxxvi.

[140] OC **17**:534 = ET **4**:37 (Calvin to de la Gaucherie, 16 May 1559).

[141] OC **17**:14 = ET **4**:41 (Calvin to Hotman, 27 May 1559).

[142] Walker 368.

[143] R.E. McGrew, *Encyclopaedia of Medical History* (London: Macmillan, 1985), 151, art. 'Influenza'.

[144] Beza OC **21**:160 = Beza ET lxxxiii.

[145] J-B Bouillaud, *Nouvelles recherches sur le rhumatisme articulaire.* (Paris: 1836).

[146] W.S.C.Copeman, *A Short History of the Gout and the Rheumatic Diseases* (Berkeley: University of California Press, 1964), 118-119. See Hippocrates, *Affections* 30 (Loeb edition **5**:53).

[147] Colladon OC **21**:89.

[148] OC **40**:21. *Lectures on Ezekiel, Prolegomena 2* (Note by Charles Jonvilliers). See Calvin Translation Society edition (Edinburgh 1849); **1**:xlvii. Calvin's exposition during his last lecture on Feb. 2nd 1564, ended at Ezekiel **20**:40. See Greef 109.

[149] Hunt 308. The General Council was the largest of the three governing councils of Geneva. It was composed of all its male citizens and met twice yearly in January and November (Parker 67).

[150] Beza OC **21**:160 = Beza ET lxxxii. These regular meetings or *congrégations* for ministers and other interested persons were begun by Calvin and Farel some time before November 1536. Farel described them in a letter which is preserved in OC **10b**:71-73 (Farel to the Ministers of Lausanne, 21 Nov. 1536). Cp Greef 117-118.

[151] Beza OC **21**:162-166 = Beza ET lxxxv-lxxxix (Last Will and Testament of Master John Calvin, 25 April 1564). See also ET **4**:365-369.

[152] Beza OC **21**:162-164 = Beza ET lxxxv-lxxxix (Calvin's farewell address to the Little Council of Geneva, 27 April 1564). See also ET **4**:369-372 and Parker 181. The Little Council was the central administrative body of the government. It was composed of twenty-five members who were elected annually each February and met for business in the City hall thrice weekly (Parker 66-67).

[153] Beza OC **21**:166-167 = Beza ET xciii-xciv (Calvin's farewell address to the ministers of Geneva, 28 April 1564). See also ET **4**:372-377.

[154] Beza OC **21**:168 = Beza ET xcvi.

[155] *Ibidem.*

[156] OC **21**:815. The actual entry in the official Register for Saturday 27 May 1564 reads as follows: 'Ce iourdhuy environ huit heures du soir le sp. Jan Calvin est allé à Dieu sain et entier grâces à Dieu de sens et entendement' (*Registre du Conseil de Genève*; fol. 48:v.

[157] OC **33**:387. Sermon No. 30 on the Book of Job.

[158] OC **20**:258 (Spina to Calvin, 15 Feb. 1564). Cp Doumergue, Caractère 21.

[159] Penning 285.

[160] T.H.L.Parker, *Portrait of Calvin* (London: SCM Press, 1954), 73.

[161] Beza OC **21**:169 = Beza ET xcvii.

[162] Cooke 66.

[163] Beza OC **21**:160 = Beza ET lxxxiii.

[164] In the Register of Deaths for the City of Geneva it is recorded that Charles de Jonvilliers, one of Calvin's former secretaries, died of '*tisique*' (i.e. *phtisique* or pulmonary tuberculosis) in the year 1590 (Vol. **21**, fol. 129. See Doumergue **3**:619. There is no corresponding record of the cause of Calvin's death because the Register was only begun in 1569, five years after he died. Pulmonary tuberculosis probably occurred frequently in what we call today the Old Town areas of such cities as Geneva and Edinburgh in the sixteenth century with their insanitary and overcrowded dwelling houses. However, it was seldom recognised until its late stages, when obvious signs of its presence appeared such as the recurrent haemoptysis suffered by Calvin, or the obvious wasting of the body implied by the use of the term *phthisis*. This term is derived from the Greek verb *phthino* meaning 'to waste away'.

[165] OC **20**:283 = ET **4**:363 (Calvin to Bullinger, 6 April 1564).

[166] Colladon OC **21**:105-106

[167] Schaff **2**:824.

[168] Walker 440. Walker reproduces a photograph of the stone on which are carved Calvin's initials, 'J.C.'.

Chapter 3

THE MEDICAL HISTORY OF JOHN KNOX

One of the most striking monuments in the city of Geneva is the large and extensive memorial to the leaders of the Reformation in Europe. This monument took eight years to complete and was finally unveiled and dedicated in the year 1917 in the midst of the First World War. The central group of statues of this monument commemorates the Swiss Reformers and includes a statue of John Knox, which is a reminder of the significant part that Knox played in the Swiss Reformation in addition to his vital role in the Reformation in Scotland.

John Knox was the last of the three great leaders of the European Protestant Reformation to die. On 18 February 1546, Martin Luther died at the age of sixty-three in Eisleben in eastern Germany of myocardial infarction, secondary to systemic hypertension.[1] John Calvin died at the age of fifty-four in Geneva on 27 May 1564 of pulmonary tuberculosis.[2]

Knox was fifty-seven years old when he died in Edinburgh on 24 November 1572. Although some specific clinical details of the cause of his death have come down to us, very few details are available of his medical history during the course of his life.

The Sources

The main primary source of our information about the life and activities of John Knox is in his own writings. These were collected and edited by David Laing in six volumes under the title *The Works of John Knox*, and published in Edinburgh over the years 1846 to 1864.

The most important and informative of these works is *The History of the Reformation of Religion within the Realm of Scotland* (to give the work its full title) of which Knox wrote the first four Books.[3] These present a vivid account of the progress of the Reformation in Scotland from its earliest stages to the Seventh General Assembly of June 25th 1564 which took place in Edinburgh. Knox himself is the central figure of these Books. Although they are often regarded as his own memoirs, they are the chronicle of a movement and not primarily an autobiography. The two striking things about the Books are the way in which the author identifies himself completely with the movement whose progress he describes, and how he always refers to himself in the third person. As the justification of the activities of the leaders of this movement, the work is not unbiased but it is, nevertheless, 'remarkably trustworthy in detail'.[4] A fifth Book was added by an unknown author or authors to bring the account down to August 1567, but its pedestrian style is not that of Knox, although it is probable that Knox collected much of the material from which Book Five was compiled.[5]

Other items of Knox's own writings include letters and pamphlets. Many of his letters have been lost, but those of his personal and family letters which have survived, reveal the human and affectionate side of the man which is often lost sight of in the controversy which surrounds him.

Another important primary source is the *Memorials of Transactions in Scotland from 1569 to 1573* which was compiled by Richard Bannatyne, who was Knox's secretary in his latter years. This work incorporates entries from Knox's journal of the events of the last years of his life, together with materials which he had collected for use in the continuation of his *History of the Reformation*. These are supplemented by entries from Bannatyne's own journal of events, notably an account of the last days of his master's life.

A second contemporary account of the last days of Knox's life also exists. This was written in Latin, while Bannatyne's journal was written in Scots. It was published in Edinburgh in 1579 by Thomas Smeton (or Smeaton), at that time the minister of Paisley and subsequently Principal of Glasgow University. It is a more verbose document than Bannatyne's *Memorials*, but no name is attached to it, although the author is said to have sat with Knox during his last illness. Laing believed that it was written by James Lawson, who succeeded Knox as minister of St Giles just two weeks before Knox died in November 1572.[6]

Family History

The name Knox is said to be derived from the Celtic word *cnoc* which means 'a small hill'. It occurs today in topographical terms such as the Knock of Crieff. Its origin as a family name presumably lies in the association of the ancestors of the Knoxes with some location in which a small hill was a characteristic feature. The site of that small hill is quite unknown, although it has been suggested that it lay in Renfrewshire, where the most noteworthy branch of the Knox family lived in the sixteenth century possessed of the lands of Knock,

Ranfurly and Craigend which were situated on the east side of the River Cart near Paisley.[7] However, although the name may have been imported into East Lothian, 'it is just as likely that the Knoxes of the county acquired their name locally', since Knox was 'descendit but of lineage small' and not connected with any distinguished family.[8]

By the time John Knox was born, his surname was a common one throughout the Scottish Lowlands. It was variously written in English or Scots, Knox, Knock or Knockes; whilst foreign writers spelt it Cnox, Cnoxus or Knoxus. As Ridley points out, its pronunciation was sufficiently close to that of the Latin words *nox* (night) and *noceus* (criminal) to provide Knox's opponents with the opportunity of making many a hostile pun at his expense. One example of this was their description of Knox as *quasi nox, a nocendo* ('like darkness from the doing of dark deeds'). Nevertheless, the initial letter K of the name appears to have been pronounced in Knox's time and not left silent as it is today, although it was sometimes omitted in spelling so that the name was written simply as Nox.[9]

Parentage

Little is known about Knox's parents and after he has left home to go to university, they disappear entirely from his story. We know that his father was called William only because this fact was recorded in the register of burgesses of the city of Geneva, when his son John was enrolled as a burgess or citizen there on 24 June 1558.[10] In this register, Knox appears as *'Jehan filz de Guillaume Cnoxe natif de Hedington en Ecosse'*.[11]

So far as his mother is concerned, we know only that her surname was Sinclair. This explains why Knox would sometimes sign his letters 'John Sinclair' when he wished to hide the identity of their writer in times of danger to his life and freedom and to those of his correspondents.[12] According to Knox's biographer, Hume Brown, this was a common practice amongst the Huguenots or French Protestants at that time.[13]

The lack of information about the early life of Knox indicates that he was of humble origin. While he 'owed nothing to the advantages of birth or fortune',[14] nevertheless he belonged to a respectable, honest and hard-working family. His father and grandfathers were tenant farmers on the East Lothian estates of the Earls of Bothwell (whose family name was Hepburn). They and their forebears stood in feudal relationship to the Earls, and some had died under their standards, probably at the Battles of Sauchieburn (1488) and Flodden (1513).[15]

We have no details of the medical history of Knox's parents, and do not know when they died, nor what may have been the cause of their deaths. It has been suggested that William Knox was amongst those slain at the Battle of Flodden in September 1513 along with Adam, the second Earl of Bothwell.[16] If this were so, then Knox at that time would be only an infant in arms or would be born posthumously.[17] Tradition has it that his mother died early in life.[18] They had only two children - John and William, his elder brother. William settled in Prestonpans and became a prosperous merchant. Along with some others, he formed a company which bought a ship and traded with England in 'all kind of goods and lawful merchandise'.[19] He had three sons, all of whom became ministers of the Church of Scotland, respectively of Cockpen (William), Kelso (Paul) and Lauder (John).[20]

Date of birth

For over four centuries it was believed that Knox was in his sixty-seventh year when he died in 1572 and so must have been born in the year 1505. This estimate of his age at death was given in Archbishop John Spottiswoode's *History of the Church of Scotland* which was written some time before the latter's death in 1639, but not published until 1655.[21] It is now recognised that this estimate was incorrect and that Spottiswoode's printer had misread the author's '57th' for '67th' and so made Knox die in his sixty-seventh year. This error was uncovered by Hay Fleming at the time of the celebration of the alleged quatercentenary of Knox's birth in 1905. Fleming pointed out that Knox's contemporaries, Sir Peter Young and Theodore Beza, said he died in his fifty-ninth year and fifty-seventh year respectively. This meant that he must have been born between 24 November 1513 and 24 November 1515, with sometime in the year 1514 being the most probable date.[22] If his father was killed at Flodden on 9 September 1513, Knox, even if he were a posthumous child, cannot have been born later than the spring or early summer of 1514. More specific than this we cannot be, although Lord Eustace Percy suggests he was born in the month of December 1513.[23]

Place of birth

The entry in the Genevan register of burgesses to which we have already referred, records that Knox was born in Haddington in Scotland. An apparently more precise reference is given in a note by Beza in his collection of portraits of Reformation leaders published in 1580, which says that Johannes Cnoxus was a native of Gifford (*Johannes Cnoxus Scotus Giffordiensis*).[24] Today this is the name of a village about four miles south of the royal burgh of Haddington, the chief town of East Lothian and the first stage on the old road from Edinburgh to London. However, the village which is today called Gifford, was previously called Bothans and only became known as Gifford about 1668, more than a century after Knox's birth.

A possible explanation of the apparent discrepancy was suggested by Dr George Barclay who was the minister of Haddington from 1722 to 1795. He pointed out that within the parish of Haddington lay two villages on the east side of the River Tyne, while the main part of the town lay on the west. Of the two villages one was called Nungate because it was built on the lands of the Abbey, and the other was called Giffordgate because it was built on the lands owned by the Gifford family. Barclay said that it was here that the Reformer was born, namely, in a house in Giffordgate. He said it was a house of but mean appearance, which was still in existence when he contributed the article on Haddington to the *Statistical Account of Scotland* in 1791.[25] The situation of this house was directly opposite the east end of the parish Church of St Mary's, but on the other side of the river. By the time the *Second Statistical Account* was compiled in 1845 the house had disappeared, but the site was still pointed out as that where the house had stood.[26] Thomas Carlyle, whose wife Jane Welsh was a native of Haddington and a descendant of John Knox through his youngest daughter Elizabeth, had a memorial oak tree planted on this site with a tablet beside it stating that this marked the site of the house in which John Knox had been born.

Education

When he was seven years old, Knox probably attended a Church song-school in Haddington where he would be taught the elements of Latin and religious knowledge, and be trained to sing in the Church choir.[27] Then at age ten he would transfer to the Burgh or Grammar School. Here he would continue to be taught Latin together with logic, science and mathematics.[28] The Latin primer in general use was still that of Donatus, the fourth century Roman grammarian, although in 1522 a new grammar had been published by John Vaus of Aberdeen and so it is possible that this new book was the one from which Knox learned his Latin grammar.[29]

In 1529 when he was fifteen years of age he went to St Andrews University to train for the Roman priesthood. Edinburgh University was not yet in existence and it is unlikely that he went to Glasgow University as was previously thought.[30] Haddington was in the diocese of St Andrews and it would be more natural for him to attend the University there. He spent his first two years studying Arts, taking his B.A. at the close of his Arts course, which would entitle him to be called 'Sir John Knox'. This was the usual designation of a secular priest who had not obtained the university distinction of Master (*Magister*) and was derived from the Latin title *Dominus*. Such a priest was often called a 'Papal knight' as opposed to a knight created by a secular authority.[31] Following this he studied the prevailing scholastic theology for three to four years and obtained his B.D. degree under John Major in St Salvator's College.[32] Major also was a native of Haddington and by that time had become one of the leading intellectual figures of Europe, and been appointed Provost or Head of this college.

According to Beza, Knox was an outstanding student at the University who was expected to outshine his teacher, John Major.[33] He had a genuine enthusiasm for knowledge which is reflected in the style and content of his writings.[34]

> As a *writer* of the old rich English tongue our Reformer has few equals and no superior. His prose is stately and full of music. Avoiding pedantry and classical and scholastic terms, he is a writer for all times, intelligible in every age, with an attractive literary excellence. In almost everything he wrote there is a touch of greatness.[35]

His language was refined and not vulgar and he used only a few Scottish words or idioms in his *History of the Reformation* and these usually when he was reporting direct speech. He spoke an anglicised Scots which was the result of his long residence in Europe and in England, his marrying into an English family and above all his intimate knowledge of the English Bible in the Genevan version of 1560, in the production of which Knox may have shared during his stay in Geneva in the years 1554, 1555 and 1588. Ninian Winzet (Wingate), one of his opponents, as he was about to debate with him in public at Linlithgow in 1559, said that he would have to use Latin in the debate as Knox had forgotten 'our auld plaine Scottis', and Winzet did not understand Knox's southern accent.[36]

Knox remained a student all his life. In December 1562, at the close of his second interview with Mary Queen of Scots, he complained that all the waiting at Court she demanded, was keeping him from his books.[37] His books constituted much the larger part of his personal property and it was with them, and with helps from the old scholastic logic and the new learning (which included the Hebrew he had acquired during 'his quiet life of study' in Geneva in 1555), that he spent hours in the preparation of the long sermons which he delivered in the course of his ministry in Edinburgh.[38]

The Public Figure

After Knox had completed his studies, he taught scholastic philosophy and theology, most probably as a regent of one of the classes in the University. He was a good teacher and his classes were popular with the students.[39] He left St Andrews University finally in 1536 and was ordained a deacon in the Roman Church on April 1st of that year. Then on Easter Eve, Saturday 15 April, he was ordained to the priesthood by William Chisholm, Bishop of Dunblane, at Haddington in the Franciscan Church of St Mary ('The Lamp of Lothian').[40] The canonical age for ordination was twenty-four years and Knox's ordination at the age of twenty-two suggests that he must have impressed the Church authorities by his ability and learning.[41]

Nothing is known of Knox's life and activity for the four years after he was ordained. He does not appear to have obtained a benefice as might have been expected. However, by 1540 he is acting as a notary apostolic, providing legal services for members of the community in and around Haddington. The name of his office means that he acted under the authority of the Church of Rome. In 1543 we find him living at Longniddry House in East Lothian as tutor to the sons of the Protestant lairds of Longniddry and Ormiston, teaching them Latin grammar and literature, a little French and some Bible and religious knowledge, using a catechism and the gospel of John.[42]

Meanwhile, significant events had been taking place on the continent of Europe, whose influence was to change the course of Knox's life and turn him into a figure of Scottish and European renown. These events were those of the rise and progress of the Reformation. Although the Reformation began with Martin Luther in Germany, it soon spread to other countries including Scotland. Its teaching entered Scotland through the east coast ports of Dundee, Montrose and Leith, carried by traders visiting Germany, France and the Low Countries, and by students returning from their studies in Continental Universities. From these coastal Scottish ports, the influence and teaching of the Reformation was spread by itinerant preachers throughout the rest of the country. One of these preachers was Thomas Gwilliam, a Court chaplain who was the former Prior of the Dominican or Blackfriars monastery at Inverness, and who had in fact been born at Athelstaneford in East Lothian.[43] When Gwilliam preached in Lothian, Knox was among his audience and he was impressed by his preaching and teaching. It was Gwilliam who first interested Knox in the Reformed Faith.[44]

However, the person most responsible for Knox's committing himself to the Reformed Faith and becoming a public figure, was Master George Wishart (1512-1546).[45] Wishart had been a schoolmaster at Montrose and had been declared a heretic for teaching the Greek New Testament in the grammar school there.[46] After spending some time in Switzerland in contact with Reformation leaders there, Wishart returned to Scotland in 1544 and in December 1545 he preached in different places in East Lothian. Knox was in close contact with him at this time and learned from him the doctrines of the Reformed Faith including those of justification by faith as the sole basis of human salvation and of the supremacy of Scripture as the sole guide of faith and life.[47] As Wishart's life was constantly in danger he always took about with him an old-fashioned two-handed sword, which Whitley suggests may have been a relic of Flodden.[48] During his preaching tour in Lothian, this sword was carried by John Knox who thus acted as his bodyguard. This meant that Knox, having in this way declared his commitment to the Reformed cause, now became a public figure and a marked man.

Although Knox was now a wanted man, he continued to act as tutor to the sons of the lairds of Longniddry and Ormiston in order to prepare them for entrance to St Andrews University. At first, wearied of the constant movement from place to place to evade capture by the Church authorities, he had thoughts of leaving Scotland for Germany where he might study at the Protestant Universities of Wittenberg or Marburg ('the schools of Germany' as he called them). However, the lairds encouraged him to remain in Scotland and continue the education of their sons. He agreed to do this, although it meant that they had to be continually on the move with him.

In April 1547, the fathers of his pupils suggested that Knox and their sons might be safer if they moved to the Castle of St Andrews. This Castle had been occupied by Protestant sympathisers since the murder there of Cardinal David Beaton, the leader of the Roman Church in Scotland, on 26 May 1546. Following this suggestion, Knox and his pupils sailed across the Firth of Forth and round the coast to St Andrews, arriving at the Castle on 10 April 1547. However, this move proved to be disastrous. On 30 July, the Castle, subjected to bombardment from without and its garrison weakened by an outbreak of bubonic plague within, fell to the French forces summoned to their aid by Mary of Guise, the Queen Dowager and the Earl of Arran, the Regent or Governor of Scotland. The 'Castilians', as its occupants were called, were carried off to France where, in violation of the agreed terms of their surrender, the nobles, lairds and those of rank were committed to the prisons of Brest, Cherbourg, Mont St Michel and Rouen, and the commoners, who included Knox, consigned to the galleys based at Nantes on the Loire or Rouen on the Seine, as captive oarsmen or *forsairs*.

The Galley-slave

The galleys were the labour camps of that period. Consignment to the galleys was regarded as the worst fate available after capital punishment and was the alternative punishment for convicts whose death sentence was commuted. Hume Brown describes service on them as 'a form of life which for unutterable horror is perhaps without parallel in the history of humanity'.[49] This was to be Knox's fate for nineteen months, on the galleys which sailed from the French ports to patrol the east coast of Scotland. These galleys were used to convoy French troopships bringing soldiers and supplies to Scotland, and to intercept any English ships which might be bringing assistance to the Reformation party there.

The average French galley was one hundred and fifty feet long with a beam of fifty feet. Such galleys stood only about six feet above the water-line and so were not very seaworthy in rough weather. This meant that they could cross the North Sea to Scotland only in summer. Each galley had a crew of about a hundred and fifty men, with an average complement of three hundred slaves or *galériens* to work the oars. From the captain's cabin at the stern ran a raised central walkway on either side of which, the benches for the oarsmen were set at right angles to the vessel's side. There were twenty-five oars on each side, each rowed by six men who were chained to each other by the neck in couples, and to their benches by leg-irons day and night. At night, the men slept on a little straw under their bench and during the day they roasted in the sun or shivered in the cold or rain according to the weather for the galleys were only partially decked. Although they had been convicted of no crime and were not even French, Knox and his colleagues found themselves rowing in the company of some of the worst criminals of France, and subject to violent ill-treatment by the officers in charge of the slaves (*comités*) and their deputies (*sous-comités*). These men carried cowhide whips by which they encouraged the rowers and enforced discipline, often quite arbitrarily and on the slightest provocation. Any rower who professed to be ill or injured was first whipped to make sure he was not malingering.[50]

When the galleys were laid up for the winter, the galley slaves had time to pursue their own interests, although still kept in chains. In Knox's case, during the second winter of his captivity when he was stationed at Rouen, he was able to edit a treatise on *Justification by Faith* which had been written by Henry Balnaves a prominent Scottish lawyer and a fellow-prisoner, who was confined in the old palace at Rouen. Balnaves was able to pass the manuscript out to Knox who divided it into chapters, wrote a summary of it and added notes and a commendatory preface to the text. This was in spite of what Knox calls with grim humour, his 'incommodity of place, as well as imbecility of mind'.[51]

It is at this stage of his life that we first come across references to Knox's health. Knox himself says little about the conditions on board the galleys. Later he speaks in a letter of the 'torments of the galleys',[52] but gives no details apart from saying that the *forsairs* were 'miserably entreated',[53] and how when he received the Balnaves manuscript just mentioned, he was at Rouen 'lying in irons, sore troubled by corporal infirmity in a galley called *Notre Dame*'.[54]

There were several possible causes of this 'corporal infirmity'. There was the heavy physical work of rowing; the cramped space and position in which that rowing had to be performed, and the frequent ill-treatment under the lash of the whips of the overseers. There was the continual exposure to the elements of sun, rain and cold, and to the insanitary conditions on board the galley which harboured rats, to say nothing of lice and other parasites. Finally, there was the grossly inadequate diet which the slaves were given. This consisted of coarse ship's biscuit and water, with a kind of porridge of oil and beans three times a week. In addition, they were given wine when they were working on land.[55]

After about a year exposed to these conditions, it is not surprising that Knox's health finally broke down. He had been a man in his early thirties and in robust health when he was first consigned to the galleys, but now he was exhausted and weakened by the severe physical work, and emaciated because of the inadequate diet. In the summer of 1548 he developed a fever and became so ill that his life was despaired of by all in the ship.[56] There is no evidence of the nature of the fever. It may have been bubonic plague for we know that there were rats on board the galleys, and that this disease had appeared amongst the occupants of the Castle before it fell to the French forces.[57] Each galley had a 'hospital' which was situated in the centre and bottom of the ship where the sick were tended by the barber-surgeon, but this was such 'a plague-stricken hole' that the sick preferred to stay at their oar rather than be put into it.[58] This would appear to confirm that bubonic plague did occur on the galleys. Another possibility is that Knox had contracted louse-borne typhus fever in view of the insanitary conditions and overcrowding on board the galleys.

In March 1549, Knox was released by the French Government after the successful negotiations of the English Government for the release of all the 'Castilians'. He arrived in England in the following month where the young Protestant King Edward VI was now on the throne. Within a few weeks of his arrival he was licensed as a preacher by the English Privy Council and appointed to be minister of the garrison and the parish of Berwick, which was described before Knox went there, as 'a town of theft, debate, hatred and all iniquity'. This strongly-fortified border town had been ceded by Scotland to England in 1482, and so was within the jurisdiction of the Church of England for Church affairs. It was here that Knox began his real work as a preacher of the Reformation, in a Church which was much too small for the large congregation of soldiers and civilians it had to accommodate at this time. After a year he was transferred to Newcastle where he preached regularly in the Parish Church of St Nicholas (now the Cathedral) and then finally to London where he served as a chaplain to King Edward VI on an annual salary of forty pounds. As one of the six Royal Chaplains he assisted in the final stages of the revision of Edward VI's Second Prayer Book (mainly the work of Thomas Cranmer) and the production of the Anglican Articles of Faith known as the Forty-two Articles (1553) which formed the basis of the later Thirty-nine Articles (1571). When Edward VI died from tuberculosis on 6 July 1553 at the age of sixteen, Knox was in Buckinghamshire as part of an itinerant preaching tour of the southern counties of England for which he had been commissioned by the Council. After two weeks he returned to London, but with the accession to the English throne of the Roman Catholic Mary Tudor later in the same month, Knox once again became a wanted man and his friends advised him to leave England. He was one of the last Protestant leaders to leave the country when, early in 1554, he crossed the English Channel to Dieppe and after a few weeks made his way to Geneva, where he met John Calvin for the first time, who introduced him to the other Swiss Reformers in Zürich and Lausanne.

It was during his ministry at Berwick that Knox made the acquaintance of the family of Richard Bowes of Aske in County Durham, who was then the Captain of Norham Castle which lay about seven miles to the west of Berwick. He became the pastor and spiritual counsellor of Mrs Elizabeth Bowes, whose fifth daughter, Marjory Joan, he later married. It was a female descendant of Mrs Bowes who in 1767 married John Lyon, the ninth Earl of Strathmore, to found the Bowes-Lyon family from which our present Queen Elizabeth is descended through her mother.[59]

The Family Man

We do not know exactly when Knox married Marjory Bowes but it was probably about Christmas 1552 that they became officially engaged, for by January 1553 he begins to write to her mother as 'mother', having previously addressed her as 'sister', and in a letter dated 20 September of that year he refers to Marjory as 'my wife'.[60] The actual marriage ceremony probably took place in the summer of 1555 when Knox visited Berwick on his way from Geneva to Edinburgh.[61]

Marjory proved to be an invaluable helpmate to Knox and he always speaks of her in terms of cordial respect and affection. In a letter written to Knox after her death, Calvin spoke of her as 'a wife the like of whom is not easily found (*uxor nactus eras cui non reperiuntur passim similes*)'.[62] In another letter, this time to Knox's friend and colleague Christopher Goodman, Calvin describes her as 'the most delightful (*suavissima*) of wives'.[63]

In July 1556 Knox returned with his new wife and mother-in-law to Geneva where he became minister of the Church of Notre Dame de la Neuve situated near St Peter's Cathedral. During their stay in Geneva, two sons were born to Marjory and her husband. Nathaniel was baptised in May 1557 and Eleazar in November of the following year.

After only about eight years of married life, Marjory Knox died in Edinburgh in December 1560 at the time when the First General Assembly of 'the Universal Kirk of Scotland' was meeting in the Magdalene Chapel in the Cowgate of Edinburgh. At this time, Knox records that 'he was in no small heaviness by reason of the late death of his dear bedfellow, Marjory Bowes'.[64] She had often acted as his secretary and some of his letters are written in her fine, clear handwriting. She was probably not much more than twenty-five years old at this time and the cause of her early death is unknown. It has been suggested that she died in childbirth or from one of the many deadly diseases prevalent in sixteenth century Europe.[65] If it was in childbirth, then the child must have been stillborn or have died soon after birth for no record of it survives.

When his wife died, their two sons were aged about three and two years respectively and although Mrs Bowes at first returned to her family in England, she came back to Edinburgh after about eighteen months to help her son-in-law care for the boys, finally returning to England when Knox remarried in 1564.[66]

Little is known about Knox's sons until they both matriculated at the University of Cambridge eight days after their father died, and were admitted to St John's College there where Thomas Lever, a former colleague of their father's at Frankfurt-on-the-Main, was then Master. In due course they graduated in Arts and became Fellows of the College. Both of them entered the ministry of the Church of England. Nathaniel died of malaria (tertian ague) in 1580 while still at college.[67] Eleazar had a brilliant academic career and in May 1587 became vicar of Clacton Magna in Essex. He died on 23 May 1591 and was buried in the chapel of St John's College. Neither son married and so with the death of Eleazar, the male line of Knox's family became extinct.

It was four years after the death of Marjory, that Knox married again, on Palm Sunday 28 March 1564. His new bride was Margaret Stewart, the daughter of Andrew, Lord Ochiltree, a descendant of James II. According to Thomas Randolph, the English ambassador, Mary Queen of Scots objected strongly to the marriage because Margaret was 'of the blood and of the name', being a distant cousin of her own.[68] Margaret was only seventeen years old and Knox was now fifty, a disparity in age which gave rise to some malicious gossip in

Edinburgh, in addition to the Queen's objection that she was marrying below her station. She proved to be a faithful and affectionate wife, although Knox makes few allusions to her in his writings. She bore him three daughters, Martha, Margaret and Elizabeth who were aged about six, four and two years when Knox died in 1572. After his death, his wife Margaret went on to outlive him by forty years, dying in 1612.

His General Health

Knox came of good farming stock in East Lothian, a fertile and prosperous area of the Scottish Lowlands. As we have already indicated, we know nothing of the health of his parents, the length of their lives or the cause of their death. Their daily life on the farm would be hard and simple and would be shared by John until he left home to go to the University of St Andrews. The fact that they were able to send him to university suggests that they did not live in the poorest of circumstances. There is no evidence to suggest that he enjoyed anything other than good health for at least the first thirty-two years of his life.

However, his biographers are divided about the strength of his constitution. Hume Brown regarded him as naturally of 'a feeble constitution',[69] but gives no evidence to support his opinion. Ridley, on the other hand, spoke of him as 'the type of man who survives a labour camp' and how when he was consigned to the galleys 'he was physically in his prime at the age of 33, and obviously robust'.[70] Reid, a recent North American biographer, also describes Knox as 'a man of considerable physical strength'.[71] Certainly he was no weakling if he could withstand a year of hard labour, ill-treatment, deprivation and malnutrition before showing signs of breaking down, and falling a victim to the infectious disease from which he nearly died.

Even after his release from the galleys in 1549, he still had the strength and energy to face a demanding career of over twenty years; a career in which he sought to carry through a heavy programme of work in the face of opposition, persecution and misrepresentation, and in which his aim was to provide his people and his country with a constitutional government, a national scheme of education and a reformed religion.

The question now arises of whether we have any record of the physical appearance of Knox which may allow us to form some opinion of the state of his health. We are fortunate in having both a description and a portrait of him.

The description was written by Sir Peter Young (1544-1628), tutor to James VI and a citizen of Edinburgh, in response to a request by Theodore Beza, a colleague of John Calvin in Geneva. In 1579,

Beza was collecting biographical information to include in a book of portraits of leaders of the Reformation and had applied to Scotland for assistance with the biography of Knox. The original of Young's letter in which he described Knox was discovered at the end of last century in the Ducal Library at Gotha in Thuringia, Germany.[72] It was written in Latin and was dated 13 November 1579. It described Knox in the following terms:

> In bodily stature he was rather below the normal height. His limbs were straight and well-proportioned; his shoulders broad; his fingers somewhat long. His head was of medium size, with black hair; his appearance swarthy, yet not unpleasant. His countenance, which was grave and stern, though not harsh, bore a natural dignity and air of authority; in anger his frown became very imperious. Under a rather narrow forehead his eyebrows rose in a dense ridge; his cheeks were ruddy and somewhat full, so that it seemed as though his eyes receded into hollows. The eyes themselves were dark blue, keen and animated. His face was somewhat long, with a long nose, a full mouth, and large lips of which the upper one was slightly the thicker. His beard was black flecked with grey, thick and falling down a hand and a half long.[73]

The date of this letter is some seven years after the death of Knox and means that Young was writing from memory, and describing Knox as he remembered him in the full vigour of his adult life.

No portrait of Knox was painted in his lifetime. The portrait which was published in Beza's *Portraits (Icones) of Illustrious Men* in 1580 was painted from memory by the Flemish artist Adrian Vaensoun, and sent by Young to Beza in Geneva along with the letter we have just quoted. It agrees with Young's description of Knox, except that the beard is too long.

The length of Knox's beard has given rise to a whole controversial literature, but it seems clear that he did not have 'a river of a beard' as Beza's portrait depicted, but only one about six inches in length.[74]

The significance of both the description and the portrait of Knox for our present purpose is that neither of them show any features which can be regarded as those of any form of ill-health.

His Clinical History

There are very few specifically clinical references in Knox's writings, and therefore also in the various volumes of biography which are based upon them. For instance, the two-volume biography of Knox by Hume Brown never mentions fever at all, and there are only two references to fever in Thomas McCrie's biography which runs to well over five hundred pages. There are some references to ill-health and ailments in both biographies, but their nature is not specified. Thus when Knox arrived in Geneva from Scotland in 1556, we read that he was then able to enjoy family life and receive the soothing care which 'his frequent bodily ailments now required',[75] but we are given no indication of what those ailments were. For our present purpose we propose to pick out what references there are to ailments in Knox's own writings or in his biographies and consider them symptomatically.

Fever

We have already mentioned the fever that accompanied the breakdown in health which Knox suffered in 1548 after a year as a galley-slave.[76] We suggested that this 'galley-fever' might have been bubonic plague or louse-borne typhus fever contracted amid the insanitary conditions aboard the galleys.

In August 1551, whilst Knox was still a minister in Newcastle, a severe outbreak of the Sweating Sickness occurred there and in Northumberland, the worst for over thirty years.[77] However, although we know that the Duke of Northumberland (John Dudley) lost his daughter in this outbreak in June 1552,[78] we have no information about whether Knox contracted this disease, although his bodily resistance to disease must have been very low at this time following his experience of the galleys.

In a letter to Mrs Anna Locke dated 2 September 1559, Knox speaks of travelling throughout the realm of Scotland in the interests of the Reformation 'notwithstanding the fevers which have vexed me for the space of a month'.[79] However, he gives no indication of the nature of these fevers but they obviously appear to have been chronic if they persisted for a month. They affected his work, but did not apparently threaten his life.

Pain

We first meet with a specific mention of pain in the year 1553 when he was in England. He had several severe attacks of 'the gravel', or the passage of kidney stones down the urinary tract producing the acute pain of renal colic. He calls this 'my old malady' and ascribes it to his confinement on the French galleys.[80] He also speaks of spending sore and dolorous nights with severe pain in his head and stomach.[81] The mention of stomach pain has led to the suggestion that Knox suffered from peptic ulcer,[82] but the mention of 'gravel' would suggest that it was more probably due to kidney stones or urinary calculi and the pain or colic they caused as they passed down the urinary tract.

This condition appears to have been common in Europe in the sixteenth century. As we have already seen in previous chapters, both

Luther and Calvin suffered from urinary calculi and their effects, which have been described by one of Knox's biographers as those of 'one of the cruellest diseases that can torture human flesh'.[83] Luther gives a dramatic account of an incident of urethral obstruction due to the impaction of urinary calculi in his urethra.[84] Calvin also provides a classic description of an attack of renal colic caused by the passage of a renal calculus down the ureter.[85] Knox's mention that the gravel began to affect him while he was confined to the galleys suggests that one predisposing factor to its development was the inadequate supply of wine or drinking water on board the galleys resulting in a state of chronic dehydration. This in turn would lead to the production and excretion of concentrated urine with the consequent predisposition to the formation of calculi in the urinary tract.

The only other type of specific pain to which Knox refers is that which occurred at the end of his life, and which appears to have been respiratory in origin. We shall consider this pain and its nature further, when we describe the last days of his life later in this study of his medical history.

Stress

Until the year 1546, when he was about thirty-two years old, Knox had lived a relatively sheltered life apparently free from stress and ill-health. However, once he committed himself to the cause of the Reformation, his life became very full of stress. He became a hunted man and the events and activities which he records in his *History of the Reformation* illustrate the stress in which he lived. We can mention only a few of these by way of illustration.

He was consigned to forced labour on the galleys which has already been described and from which he nearly died. He engaged in protracted negotiations with political leaders concerning religious freedom, some of whom were fickle and untrustworthy. On one occasion in December 1563, he was arraigned before the Queen and her Privy Council on a trumped-up charge of high treason but was acquitted.[86] At various times in his life he had a heavy programme of preaching and writing. He describes this as his 'daily labour' and that he finds that 'nothing is more contrarious to my health than writing'.[87]

Much of this writing arose from his desire to see that the newly-reformed Church was provided with a statement of its basic doctrines, a document setting out its Presbyterian constitution and a book of Common Order for the guidance of its worship. The preparation of these documents, drawn up by Knox in consultation with his colleagues, was then followed by their submission to the new Church authorities to gain their acceptance. He was busy on the task of compiling his *History of the Reformation* up to the months before he died and as we have already mentioned, he left material for a fifth Book of that

History, which he did not live to see completed. This material was left for his secretary Richard Bannatyne to deal with.

When we realise too, how much travelling around Scotland he did in order to preach and to establish new congregations on the Reformed pattern, we can understand what lay behind his comment in a letter written in September 1559 to his correspondent Mrs Anna Locke that 'Time to me is so precious, that only with great difficulty can I steal one hour in eight days, either to satisfy myself, or to gratify my friends'.[88] In the following month he writes to another correspondent, Gregory Raylton, 'in twenty-four hours, I have not four free to natural rest and ease of this wicked carcass... I write with sleeping eyes'.[89] In addition to his writing, his study and his preaching, he carried a heavy pastoral responsibility for the counselling and care of those who formed his congregations in the different places in which he ministered.

Not only was he concerned with Church affairs, he was also involved in affairs of State arising from his desire to see the absolute monarchy of the Stewart dynasty replaced by a constitutional government in which the people were represented. Implied in this desire, as we have already mentioned, was the establishment of a scheme of universal compulsory education, a scheme which was thwarted when the Scottish nobles insisted on appropriating the lands and revenues of the Roman Church, with the result that these could not be used to establish schools and train and pay teachers, which was part of Knox's plan.

It is obvious that in all these areas of his interest and activity, he would run into a great deal of opposition and make a large number of enemies, which did not make life any easier for him. Undoubtedly, Knox lived a life full of stress which must have produced periods of anxiety and depression. However, there is no suggestion that these symptoms became permanent and established as an anxiety state or depressive illness respectively. They were the normal and transient responses to the various events of Knox's life. He met each reverse with fearlessness and courage based on his steadfast faith in God, in his own call to be God's servant, and in the ultimate triumph of what he believed to be God's cause.

Exhaustion

When Knox finally reached England after his nineteen months of captivity and forced labour on the French galleys, he must have been in a very exhausted and debilitated condition. He then ministered in Berwick and Newcastle for three years where he was very happy and able to engage in what he calls 'bodily exercise' by which he meant the outdoor sports of bowls, archery and perhaps hunting.[90]

Although Knox may never have recovered his full strength after his imprisonment in the galleys, he was still able to undertake a life full of strenuous activity. However, there were times of weakness and exhaustion associated with his old trouble, the gravel, and with his frequent bodily ailments, whatever they may have been, perhaps attacks of fever both acute and chronic contracted on his journeys round Scotland. In addition there were periods of intense political and religious activity which left him exhausted, especially after Mary Queen of Scots returned to Scotland to claim her throne in 1561. References to his weakness and exhaustion begin to appear in his letters from this time onwards and he begins to long for his long battle to end. Eventually, to these causes of weakness and exhaustion was added the approach of old age which appears to have begun earlier in the sixteenth century than it does today, so that Hume Brown can say that in 1554 when Knox was about forty years old, he was 'on the verge of old age'.[91]

His Last Years

On 7 July 1559 Knox had been elected minister of the Collegiate Church of St Giles which was the parish Church of Edinburgh, and the opening of the year 1570 found him still in that position. He was, however, becoming increasingly exhausted because of the heavy pastoral and political workload he was still called upon to carry. As Hume Brown puts it, 'the weary consent to circumstance that sooner or later comes to most men, never came to Knox'.[92] He remained active to the end.

The year 1570

In October 1570, Knox suffered a stroke, which Bannatyne in his journal describes as 'a kind of Apoplexia, called by the physicians Resolution, whereby the perfect use of his tongue was stopped'. Both these words are used by the ancient medical authors for the sudden appearance of paralysis of one side of the body.[93]

The first question about Knox's stroke concerns its cause. Of the three classical causes of stroke we may dismiss cerebral embolism as unlikely in the apparent absence of any evidence of a possible source of an embolus. This leaves us with a choice between cerebral haemorrhage and cerebral thrombosis, of which cerebral thrombosis appears to be more probable.

The next question is: Which side of his body was affected? There are two possible clues to the answer to this question in the information available. The first one is in the observation by Bannatyne that when Knox suffered his stroke, 'the perfect use of his tongue was stopped'. The centre for verbal speech (Broca's area) lies in the frontal cortex of the left cerebral hemisphere and a loss of speech would normally mean that the thrombosis had affected this area and that the paralysis was on the right side of the body. However, Bannatyne does not speak of a loss of speech (*aphasia*) but of speech that was not perfect because of some interference with the use of the tongue which is one of the peripheral organs of speech (*dysarthria*). The result of this would be a decreased clarity of Knox's articulation and enunciation in normal speaking and preaching. Such an interference could be due to facial paralysis, which affected the movement of the tongue because of the weakness of the muscles on one side of the mouth. Such interference could occur, no matter which side of the face was paralysed. This first clue is therefore ambivalent since it can be explained in terms of a cerebral thrombosis on either side of the brain.

The second clue is found in the continued ability of Knox to write after his stroke and until shortly before his death. On the presumption that he was right-handed, this would mean that any paralysis affected the left-hand side of his body (and therefore the thrombosis would have been on the right-hand side of his brain). He may of course have been left-handed, but such a feature would have been seized on by his enemies anxious to discredit him by making him out to be an abnormal and demonic personality and there is no evidence that this was done. Also, it is possible that he had to resort permanently to dictation to his secretary after his stroke, but again there is no evidence of this. In fact, we find him speaking of putting his 'hand to the pen' in the introductory sentences to a document published in 1572.[94] This indicates that he had not lost his ability to write after his stroke in October 1570.

Such evidence as there is, therefore, suggests that Knox had a right-sided cerebral thrombosis with a consequent left-sided hemiparesis or paralysis of the body.

The next question concerns the severity of the stroke: Was it minor or major in degree? Bannatyne tells us that Knox confounded all the rumours about the severe degree of his disability for 'within few days... he convalescet and so returned to his exercise of preaching at least upon the Sunday'.[95] This suggests that the stroke should be regarded as a minor one.

The evidence we have examined so far does not suggest that Knox had any residual paralysis following his stroke. However, Charles McCrie maintained that the stroke left him with some degree of disablement of one hand and one foot. He finds confirmation of this in two phrases which Knox used in his writings.[96]

With regard to the hand: in signing a document in January 1571 Knox said that he signed 'with my dead hand and a glad heart praising God', i.e. for the content of the document.[97] McCrie suggested this meant that his hand was paralysed. However, it seems clear that he signed his name with his 'dead hand', which could not therefore be regarded as paralysed.

The second phrase occurs at the end of one of Knox's letters where he signs himself as 'John Knox, with his one foot in the grave'.[98] Again, McCrie takes this to mean that he suffered from paralysis of one lower limb as a result of the stroke. However, the date of this letter is 2 January 1569, which is nearly two years before the stroke occurred.

In this connection, if we examine the usage of the adjective 'dead' in Knox's writings in relation to himself or his person, we find that this usage is usually metaphorical rather than literal. In a document of 1572 we find him referring to 'my half-dead tongue'.[99] This cannot mean he had some paralysis of the tongue, for he continued to preach with as great vehemence and zeal as ever he did, until about two weeks before he died in the November of that year. At the end of a letter dated 26 May 1572, i.e. about three months before he returned to Edinburgh to resume his ministry in St Giles, he describes himself as 'lying in St Andrews, half-dead'.[100] Finally, in his last will and testament drawn up in Edinburgh and dated 13 January 1572, Knox speaks of himself as 'a dead man for almost two years past'.[101]

It would appear reasonable to conclude that when Knox speaks in these terms about himself, he is referring not to his literal death, but to his physical exhaustion and weakness. His stroke may not have left him with any marked residual paralysis, but it had made him much weaker than he was before. Following his stroke, he was now able to preach only on Sundays and not at all during the week as his previous custom had been. Also, when he went to St Giles to preach at noon each Sunday he now had to be helped across the street and up into the pulpit.[102]

The year 1571

In 1571 it became obvious that because of his increasing physical weakness and because of the political situation in Edinburgh, Knox should leave the city. In April an unsuccessful attempt on his life had alarmed his friends, but he was still very reluctant to go. Finally, on 30 April a proclamation came out from the Castle, which was held for the Queen by Sir William Kirkaldy of Grange, that all Queen Mary's enemies must leave the City of Edinburgh within six hours, and although he protested, this really gave Knox no choice but to leave. He left on 5 May, crossed the Forth at Leith three days later and then proceeded by short and easy stages across Fife to St Andrews, accompanied by his wife Margaret and their three small daughters together with Bannatyne, Knox's faithful secretary. They arrived in

St Andrews at the beginning of July and were accommodated in the *Novum Hospitium* of the Priory near St Leonard's College.[103]

On 5 August 1571, the Twenty-sixth General Assembly met at Stirling, but Knox was too weak to attend. In a letter he wrote to the Assembly, he spoke of 'the daily decay of natural strength which threatens my certain and sudden departure from the misery of this life'.[104]

Even though he was so weak and ill at this time, Knox preached every Sunday in the parish Church of Holy Trinity, expounding the book of the prophet Daniel, applying the words of the prophet to the circumstances of the time.[105] In his congregation was a young theological student called James Melville, who was the nephew of Andrew Melville, the joint architect with Knox of Presbyterianism in Scotland.[106] James was fifteen years old at the time and kept a diary in which he recorded his impression of Knox as he preached. He wrote about Knox in his diary as follows:

> I saw him every day of his preaching go carefully and slowly, with a fur of marten-skin about his neck, a staff in one hand, and good godly Richard Bannatyne, his servant, supporting his other arm, from the Abbey to the parish Kirk; and by the said Richard and another servant, lifted up to the pulpit, where he behoved to lean at his first entry; but, ere he had done with his sermon he was so active and vigorous that he was like to break the pulpit in pieces and fly out of it.[107]

Although his body was weak, Knox's mind was still acute and active. His preaching could still fascinate and thrill his hearers, as Melville testifies. Melville used to take a notebook and pen to Church to record Knox's sermons, but he found that as the sermon proceeded he became so enthralled and excited that his note-taking became impossible because he was unable to hold his pen steady.[108]

The year 1572

Knox's bodily strength was now declining fast. At the end of the letter dated 26 May 1572 which we have already quoted, he describes himself as 'lying in St Andrews, half dead'.[109] On 12 July he confesses that 'as the world is weary of me, so am I of it', and seven days later he writes that 'out of bed, and from my book, I come not but once in the week' and that was to preach.[110] However, even in bed he still continued to study and to write. In this closing year of his life, Knox completed the fourth book of his *History of the Reformation* as we have already mentioned, and issued his last publication, a forty-page pamphlet in answer to a letter written from Paris by a Scottish Jesuit professor of theology called James Tyrie to his brother David, who was a Protestant laird in Perthshire. The brother had sent the letter to

Knox for him to reply to it. In the preface to this pamphlet, Knox says that he is writing it in 'these dolorous days, after that I have taken goodnight of the world'.[111]

Meanwhile, the situation in Edinburgh had improved and on 4 August, two commissioners were sent to St Andrews with a letter signed by members of the congregation inviting Knox to return to St Giles because John Craig, his successor there, had been translated to Montrose as the result of his unpopularity amongst the members of the congregation. In spite of his great weariness, Knox readily agreed and set off by ship for Edinburgh on 17 August, landing at Leith on the 23rd where he rested for a few days. Reaching Edinburgh, he took up residence with his family in a new home in the High Street hard by the Netherbow, the house known today as 'John Knox House', which is situated within sight of St Giles.[112]

On Sunday 31 August, Knox preached once again in the great Church of St Giles. The acoustics in St Giles had never been good, but his voice was now so weak that few of the congregation could hear him. On the Sundays which still remained to him, he arranged to preach in the smaller building of the Outer Tolbooth, which had been created about 1564 by dividing off the west end of the nave of the Cathedral. The building so created had two storeys; the lower one was used as a Law court and Council chamber, and the upper one for worship. It was in this much smaller accommodation of the Upper Tolbooth that Knox chose to preach his final series of sermons.[113]

About six weeks before Knox died, we have a description of him written by Sir Henry Killigrew, the newly-appointed English ambassador to the Scottish court. It was contained in a letter from Killigrew to his superiors in London, Lord Burghley (William Cecil) and the Earl of Leicester. The ambassador reported as follows:

> John Knox is now so feeble as scarce can he stand alone, or speak to be heard of any audience; yet doth he every Sunday cause himself to be carried to a place where a certain number do hear him and doth preach with the same vehemence and zeal that he ever did.[114]

Although he could still preach with great energy as Killigrew has described, he was quite unable to cope with the pastoral work demanded of him and so a colleague was sought for him, to help in the work of the parish.

On Sunday, 9 November, Knox preached his last sermon and performed his last public duty. Having preached the sermon at the service in the Upper Tolbooth, he proceeded into the great Church where he was helped up into the pulpit and inducted James Lawson, the Vice-Principal of Aberdeen University, to be his colleague and successor as the minister of St Giles. At the close of the service he pronounced his blessing on the people. Then, leaning on his staff, he walked slowly back to his house near the Netherbow, escorted by almost the whole congregation, never to emerge from his house alive again.[115]

His Last Days

We have already had occasion to refer to the journal which was kept by Knox's secretary, Richard Bannatyne, and incorporated in his *Memorials of Transactions in Scotland*. We are indebted to this journal for the day-to-day account it provides of the last two weeks of Knox's life on earth.[116]

On Tuesday, 11 November 1572, Knox had a severe fit of coughing and brought up a great deal of phlegm, which left him very breathless.[117] His friends 'advised him to call for the assistance of physicians, particularly of Dr Preston. He readily complied, saying, that he was unwilling either to despise or neglect ordinary means, although he knew that the Lord would soon put an end to his warfare'.[118] After this he rapidly grew weaker and by Thursday he was too ill to continue his daily reading of passages from the Bible. From this time on, his wife and Bannatyne took turns to read to him such passages of Scripture as he asked them to read each day. On the Friday he was confused, for he got up from his bed saying he must go to St Giles and preach, thinking it was Sunday.

On several days he was visited by friends and public figures and was even able to sit at table with them. At his request, the Kirk Session of St Giles visited him on Monday the 17th, but the exertion of addressing the elders and deacons was too much and after this 'he became much worse; his difficulty in breathing increased, and he could not speak without great and obvious pain'.[119] Conscious that the end was not far off, on Friday the 21st he asked Bannatyne to order the wooden coffin or 'kist' in which he would be buried.[120] The next day he entertained some friends to supper and sat with them at table. On Sunday the 23rd 'he breathed with greater difficulty' and it was obvious to those who were with him that his death was not far off.[121]

On Monday 24 November, about ten o'clock in the morning, he got up and dressed and sat in a chair for about half-an-hour. He then returned to bed. When Robert Campbell, one of those who were sitting by his bedside asked him if he had any pain, Knox replied, 'It is no painful pain, but such a pain as, I trust, shall put an end to this battle'.[122]

About five o'clock he asked his wife to read the fifteenth chapter of First Corinthians and then the seventeenth chapter of John's gospel. Of this latter chapter he said it was 'where I cast my first anchor'.[123] After his wife had read to him, he fell into a deep sleep.

When he awoke he lay quiet for some hours, occasionally asking for his lips to be moistened with a little weak ale. At half-past ten the company had family worship in which his physician Dr Preston joined, and which Knox indicated that he had heard by raising his hand. About eleven he gave a long sigh and a sob, and suddenly said, 'Now it is come', and died peacefully, without any struggle or obvious pain.[124]

He was buried on Wednesday, 26 November, in the Churchyard on the south side of St Giles, which at that time extended from the Church southwards down to the Cowgate. This Churchyard was completely covered over in 1633 when Parliament House and other buildings were erected on the site, and so the grave is no longer identifiable.

The great crowd of mourners was led from the house to the graveside by James Douglas, the fourth Earl of Morton, who had been elected Regent on the very day of Knox's death. Morton was known for his laconic manner of speech,[125] and after the grave was filled in, he uttered his memorable eulogy, 'Here lies one who neither feared nor flattered any flesh'.[126]

The Cause of Death

Knox died in his fifty-eighth year. For the last twenty-five years of his life he had carried an extremely demanding burden of ecclesiastical, political and pastoral responsibility which grew heavier as the years passed. During those years he contracted fevers whose nature is unknown, but which could have included malaria (tertian ague), a disease which caused the death of his son Nathaniel in Cambridge in 1580. He had attacks of renal colic and experienced periods of intense stress and physical weakness. In his fifty-sixth year Knox appears to have had a mild stroke, probably due to a cerebral thrombosis.

Our final question in this description of his medical history concerns the cause of his death. It has been suggested that he had a second stroke some two years after his first one and that this was the cause of his death.[127] This seems unlikely. The clinical features of his terminal illness are not those of cerebrovascular disease, but of respiratory disease. These clinical features may be summarised as cough, breathlessness, pain and increasing weakness.

Cough is only mentioned at the onset of the disease on Tuesday 11 November, when it was described as producing a great deal of phlegm and leaving Knox breathless and very weak.[128] On the other hand, the accounts of his last days mention his breathlessness on several occasions, particularly after entertaining the many visitors who came to see him. The exertion of speaking to the Kirk Session of

St Giles when the members visited him at his request, increased his breathlessness and made speaking painful.[129] After the service at St Giles on the Sunday immediately before his death, some of the congregation visited Knox, and Bannatyne tells us that they 'seeing him draw his breath so shortly, asked him if he had any pain'. Knox's answer to their question was, 'I have no more pain than he that is now in heaven'.[130] We have already mentioned how on the following day, which was the day on which he died, he assured his friend Robert Campbell that it was not a painful pain he had for 'he did not consider nor feel that to be pain which should put an end to so many distresses, and be the beginning of eternal joy'.[131]

During the two weeks or so following the onset of his illness, Knox became gradually physically weaker and Smeton notes how extremely attentive his wife was to him in his weakness.[132] He became unable to continue his regular daily reading of the Bible and others took turns to read to him.[133]

The clinical picture of Knox's illness which emerges from this description includes all the major symptoms of respiratory disease, except that of haemoptysis. This suggests that he died from a lower respiratory tract infection, probably acute bronchopneumonia.

While the immediate cause of death may have been acute bronchopneumonia, Knox's elderly age and his extreme exhaustion predisposed him to the development of this disease and to the fatal outcome to which it often leads in older people. Once he had become a public figure, his life had been mainly one of ceaseless activity and unremitting toil. As a result he died an utterly exhausted man. He had proved himself to be a great Christian leader and a statesman who became 'the reformer of his Church's faith and the assertor of his country's liberty'.[134] He had exhausted himself in his battle for the political, social and, above all, the religious freedom of his people and his country.

Knox may not have left much in the way of medical records from which we can reconstruct his medical history, but he left his people a national and religious legacy on which they could build the future freedom and progress of their country. The influence of this legacy can still be seen in the life, character, literature and institutions of Scotland today.

NOTES AND REFERENCES
TO CHAPTER 3

Key to authors and sources quoted

Bannatyne = R.Bannatyne, *Memorials of Transactions in Scotland 1569-1573*, edited by Robert Pitcairn (Edinburgh: Bannatyne Club, 1836).

Brown = P.H.Brown, *John Knox: A Biography* (London: A & C Black, 1895), 2 vols.

Calderwood = D.Calderwood, *The History of the Kirk of Scotland* (Edinburgh: Wodrow Society, 1842-1849), 8 vols. This work was originally written about 1650.

Cowan = H.Cowan, *John Knox: The Hero of the Scottish Reformation* (New York: G.P.Putnam & Sons, 1905).

Dickinson = W.C.Dickinson (ed), *John Knox's History of the Reformation in Scotland* (London: Thomas Nelson, 1949), 2 vols. In this edition the spelling has been modernised throughout, but vernacular words which are still in current use at the present day have been retained.

D.N.B. = *Dictionary of National Biography*, edited by Sidney Lee (London: Smith, Elder & Co., 1892-1893).

Lorimer = P.Lorimer, *John Knox & the Church of England* (London: Henry S. King & Co., 1875).

Mason = R.A.Mason (ed), *John Knox and the British Reformations* (Aldershot: Ashgate, 1998).

McCrie = T.McCrie, *Life of John Knox* (Edinburgh: Blackwood, 1840).

McCrie, *Icones* = C.G.McCrie (ed), *Beza's Icones: Contemporary Portraits of Reformers of Religion and Letters* (London: Religious Tract Society, 1909). Charles Greig McCrie was the grandson of Thomas McCrie, the biographer of Knox.

Melville = J.Melville, *The Diary of Mr James Melville 1556-1601* (Edinburgh: Bannatyne Club, 1829).

Percy = E.Percy, *John Knox* (London: Hodder & Stoughton, 1937).

Reid = W.S.Reid, *Trumpeter of God: A Biography of John Knox* (New York: Scribners, 1974).

Ridley = J.G.Ridley, *John Knox* (Oxford: Clarendon Press, 1968).

Shaw = D.Shaw (ed), *John Knox: A Quatercentenary Reappraisal* (Edinburgh: St Andrew Press, 1975).

Smeton = *The Account of Knox's Last Illness and Death* published by Thomas Smeton (or Smeaton) in 1579 and included by Laing in Works **6**:649-660. See Reference 6 below.

Works = D.Laing, *The Works of John Knox* (Edinburgh: Wodrow Society, 1846-1864). Volumes 1 & 2 were edited by D.Laing and Volumes 3-6 by T.G.Stevenson. These volumes were reprinted in 1895 by James Thin, Edinburgh. Laing was librarian of the Signet Library in Edinburgh from 1837 to 1878 and secretary to the Bannatyne Club until its demise in 1861.

Whitley = E.Whitley, *Plain Mr Knox* (London: Skeffington, 1960).

[1]   J.Wilkinson, 'The Medical History of Martin Luther' in *Proc R Coll Physicians Edinb* (1996) **26**:128-129. See page 35 of this present volume.

[2]   J.Wilkinson, 'The Medical History of John Calvin' in *Proc R Coll Physicians Edinb* (1992) **22**:379-380. See page 75 of this present volume.

[3]   There have been several editions of Knox's *History of the Reformation* including those by David Buchanan (1644), David Laing (1864) and William Croft Dickinson (1949). A new edition is at present in preparation (2000). For a short summary of the work see David Murison in Shaw 42-50. The four books of the History were written in the order II, III, I, & IV and not in the order they are found in today (*Ibidem* 42).

[4]   W.C.Dickinson, *A New History of Scotland* (London: Thomas Nelson, 1961), **1**:319, note 2. Gordon Donaldson in Shaw (18) points out that Knox was the first figure in Scottish history for whom sufficient material still exists to provide a rounded picture of the life and personality of a particular individual. However, there is still controversy about the nature of *The History of the Reformation*. For a recent brief review of the nature of this work, ranging from Hume Brown's description of it as Knox's 'own biography writ large' (Brown **3**:31) to Worwald's happier characterisation of it as 'an odyssey of the people of God', see James Kirk in Mason 14-16.

[5]   Dickinson, **1**:xciii-xcv. Both Richard Bannatyne, Knox's secretary, and David Buchanan, the editor of the 1644 edition of Knox's *History of the Reformation*, have been suggested as the author, but both are excluded by the style of writing of the book. See Works **2**:468.

[6]   Works **6**:645-660. The introduction to this account states that it was 'drawn up by a pious and learned man, who sat by Knox during his sickness until his latest breath' (649). Laing believed that this man was James Lawson, Knox's colleague at St Giles (648). The English translation of the Latin text of this account was published in 1802, probably the work of Thomas McCrie, Knox's biographer (646).

[7]   This statement about John Knox's lineal connection with the Renfrewshire family of Knox was first made in print by David Buchanan in the account of *The Life and Death of John Knox* which he prefixed to his edition of Knox's *History of the Reformation* (Edinburgh: Robert Bryson, 1644). The statement will be found on page ii of the 1732 edition. Although McCrie accepts it on the first page of his biography of Knox, Hume Brown (**1**:5) dismisses it as lacking evidence and not worth serious consideration.

[8]   The remark about Knox's lineage was made by his contemporary John Davidson in 1573, according to Laing in Works **6**:xv. On the name of Knox see J.H.Jamieson, 'John Knox and East Lothian' in *Transactions of the East Lothian Antiquarian and Field Naturalist Society* (1938) **3**:51.

[9]   Ridley 14.

[10]   Brown **1**:4 note 2, which also said that he had a son Nathaniel (Works **6**:xvii).

[11]   Brown **1**:10.

[12]   To a letter written by Knox to Mrs Janet Adamson and Mrs Janet Henderson from Lyons in 1557 (Letter XXXV), an early annotator added the following comment after Knox's signature as John Sinclair: 'This was his mother's surname which he wrote in time of trouble'. See Works **4**:225 & 245.

[13]   Brown **1**:8 note 1.

[14]   Brown **1**:8.

[15]   Brown **1**:5. See also Works **2**:323 & Dickinson **2**:38.

[16]   Works **6**:xvi; Ridley 13. See also Whitley 17: 'We hear of no younger brothers and sisters, which strengthens the possibility that it was the father who was killed at Flodden'.

[17]   J.M.Anderson, *New Light on John Knox* (Edinburgh: Miniprint Publishers, 1979), second edition, 1.

[18]   *Ibidem* 3.

[19]   Works **6**:lxxv.

[20]   Works **6**:lxxv-lxxviii. See also W.Crawford, *Knox Genealogy* (Edinburgh: G.P. Johnstone, 1896), Appendix II: 'The Descendants of William Knox'.

[21]   J.Spottiswoode, *History of the Church of Scotland* (Edinburgh: Bannatyne Club, 1850) **2**:180.

[22]   Cowan 22, note 1. On the date of Knox's birth see D.Hay Fleming in *The Scotsman* of 27 May 1904 and *The Bookman* of 1905. For a more recent detailed discussion see Ridley 531- 534: Appendix I: 'The Date of Knox's Birth'.

[23]   Percy 9.

[24] Brown **1**:10. The clearest account of the place of Knox's birth is J.Richardson, 'The present state of the question, "Where was John Knox born?"' in *Proceedings of the Society of Antiquaries of Scotland* (1857-58) **3**:52-59. Richardson was the procurator-fiscal in Haddington when he wrote this article.

[25]   J.Sinclair (ed), *The Statistical Account of Scotland 1773- 1794* (Wakefield: EP Publishing Ltd 1975) vol.2, The Lothians: section vi:504. This is a reissue of the original edition of this volume first published in 1791.

[26]   J.H.Jamieson, 'John Knox and East Lothian' in *Transactions of the East Lothian Antiquarian and Field Naturalist Society* (1938) **3**:63-65. See also Cowan 25-29.

[27]   Ridley 15.   [28]   Brown **1**:18-19.   [29]   Ridley 15.

[30]   McCrie 2; Brown **1**:20; Ridley 535: Appendix II: 'Knox's University'.

[31]   Works **1**:555-558: Appendix XIV: 'On the Title of Sir, applied to Priests'. See also Brown **1**:59; Dickinson **1**:xxxii   note 2.

[32]   Ridley 17. However, Dickinson says 'he does not appear to have taken a degree' (**1**:xxxii. Cp Whitley 16). The records of St Andrews University show

that this was not uncommon at this time. Thus from 1513 to 1579, out of one thousand students each year, an average of only twenty-six took an ordinary degree and only ten took a master's degree. See J.M.Anderson, op. cit., 2.

[33] Ridley 17; T.Beza, *Icones* (Geneva: John Laonium, 1580), sig. Ee3.

[34] Brown **1**:29.

[35] K.Hewat, *Makers of the Scottish Church at the Reformation.* (Edinburgh: Macniven & Wallace, 1920), 17. 'In language and in style the *History* is a masterpiece, written by a man who could marshal words to meet his mood': Dickinson **1**:lxxix. Knox has been described as 'the first, almost the only, great prose writer in the vernacular' by Aeneas Mackay in D.N.B. **31**:308, art. 'Knox, John'. Nevertheless, David Murison (in Shaw 40), editor of the *Scottish National Dictionary 1946-1976*, says that Knox 'never writes pure Scots'. Murison also comments that the Geneva Bible which became the standard version for Scotland after the Reformation was 'the chief cause incidentally of the progressive anglicisation of the old Scots language'.

[36] Hewat, op. cit., 16.

[37] Works **2**:334; Dickinson **2**:46; McCrie 236.

[38] A.T.Innes, *John Knox* (Edinburgh: Oliphant, Anderson & Ferrier, 1896), 145. In a letter from St Andrews written to Mrs Anna Locke in London, Knox asks her to send him copies of two new publications by Calvin, the second edition of his commentary on Isaiah and the definitive Latin edition of his Institutes, both of which appeared in 1559, together with copies of any other books 'that be new and profitable' and he would refund their cost to her. See Works **6**:101 (Letter XLV: Knox to Mrs Locke, 18th November 1559).

[39] McCrie 8.

[40] Whitley 18. The Church was called The Lamp of Lothian (*Lucerna Laudoniae*) because when its lofty choir was lit up at night, it could be seen for miles around. See J.Miller, *The Lamp of Lothian or The History of Haddington* (Haddington: James Allan, 1844), 384.

[41] Ridley 17-18.

[42] Works **1**:185-186; Dickinson **1**:82; Ridley 26.

[43] Works **1**:95; Dickinson **1**:42; Cowan 53; Ridley 31.

[44] Calderwood **1**:155-156; see also Works **1**:42.

[45] Works **1**:125; Dickinson **1**:60.

[46] Cowan 56-60; Percy 20. Montrose was the first place in Scotland where Greek was taught in a grammar school. This was due to the encouragement of John Erskine, the laird of Dun near Montrose. See J.S.McEwen in R.S.Wright (ed), *Fathers of the Kirk* (London: Oxford University Press, 1960), 19. See also J.L.Watson, *Knox and the Reformation Times in Scotland* (Glasgow: Dunn & Wright, 1890), 25 & 41.

[47] Works **1**:137; Dickinson **1**:67.

[48] Whitley 23.   [49] Brown **1**:81.

[50] Cowan 83; Reid 55-57. See also Jean Marteilhe, *Memoirs of a Protestant condemned to the Galleys of France for his Religion.* Translated by Oliver

Goldsmith (London: Religious Tract Society, 1866). The original French edition of this book was published in 1704.

[51] Works **1**:225 & **3**:4,12-22. Cp Dickinson **1**:xxxiv and Ridley 75-78.

[52] Works **6**:104 (Letter XLVII: Knox to Mrs Locke from St Andrews, 31 December 1559). See also Brown **2**:66. Mrs Anna Locke was the wife of Henry Locke, a Protestant and a wealthy mercer of London's Cheapside. Cp Lorimer 147 & 186; Ridley 246-248 and Rupp in Shaw 13. For the details of Henry Locke see D.N.B. **34**:91-92, art. 'Lok, Lock or Locke, Henry' by Shane Leslie.

[53] Works **1**:206; Dickinson **1**:97. See also Works **1**:349.

[54] Works **3**:8 (Epistle of Knox to the Congregation of the Castle of St Andrews 1548).

[55] Ridley 67; T.M.Lindsay, *A History of the Reformation* Edinburgh: T.& T.Clark, 1908), **2**:286.

[56] This attack of fever appears to have occurred when Knox's galley was lying off the Scottish coast between Dundee and St Andrews on the second occasion on which the galleys returned to Scotland. See Works **1**:228; Dickinson **1**:109; McCrie 43; Brown **1**:85.

[57] Brown **1**:80; Cowan 81.

[58] D.Macmillan, *John Knox: A Biography* (London: Andrew Melrose 1905), 37.

[59] Whitley 48. Another connection which resulted from the marriage of Knox to Marjory Bowes was with the family of John Wycliffe, the fourteenth century Reformer. Mrs Bowes' sister was married to Harry Wycliffe, a descendant of the English Reformer. See Works **3**:350 (Letter III: Knox to Mrs Bowes from Newcastle, 26 February 1553). See also Lorimer 164.

[60] Works **3**:376 (Letter XVII: Knox to Mrs Bowes probably from London, 20 September 1553). In the same year, Knox addresses a letter from Newcastle to 'Dear mother and spouse'. See Works **3**:369 (Letter XV: Knox to Mrs Bowes, Jan. 1553).

[61] Cowan 134; Ridley 140-143.

[62] *Johannes Calvini Opera* (Brunswick: Schwelschke, 1863-1900), **18**: cols. 433-434 (Letter 3377: Calvin to Knox, 23 April 1561). English translation in Works **6**:123-124.

[63] *Ibidem* cols. 434-436 (Letter 3378: Calvin to Goodman of the same date. English translation in Works **6**:125). Knox himself in his will drawn up on 13 May 1572, spoke of Marjory as 'the dearest mother... of blessed memory' of his two sons, Nathaniel and Eleazar (Works **6**:lvi-lvii).

[64] Works **2**:138; Dickinson **1**:351.

[65] Ridley 143.

[66] Ridley 384; Works **6**:141-142 (Letter LXVI: Thomas Randolph to Sir William Cecil from Berwick, 4 August 1562). The older view was that after the death of her daughter Marjory, Mrs Bowes returned to Northumberland taking her two grandsons with her and it was from here that they went up to St John's College in Cambridge. See Cowan 391 and Works **6**:lxiii.

[67] W.Crawford, *Knox Genealogy* (Edinburgh: G.P.Johnstone, 1896), 3.

[68] Works **6**:533 (Letter LXXIII: Thomas Randolph to Sir William Cecil from Edinburgh, 18 March 1564). By this the Queen meant that Margaret was of

the royal House of Stewart. Donaldson (in Shaw 29) suggests that the fact that some four years separated the death of his first wife from his second marriage shows that the scurrilous tales about his ongoings which his enemies put about, are so completely out of character as to be discounted.

[69] Brown **1**:85. See also Smeton 649. Smeton speaks of Knox having 'a frail and weak body', but this is a description of Knox in his old age, not very long before his death.

[70] Ridley 68.

[71] Reid 32.

[72] Brown **2**:322-324. Brown gives the original Latin version of the letter.

[73] Dickinson **1**:lxxxvii. To this description of Knox we should add his sense of humour which was 'one of his most deep-rooted characteristics' according to Ridley 161. Cp Gordon Donaldson in Shaw 31.

[74] Whitley 29; Brown **2**:320-324; Ridley, Frontispiece and portrait opposite 64. The most genuine portrait of Knox is probably that originally labelled by Beza in his *Icones* as that of William Tyndale and reproduced facing page 29 in McCrie, *Icones* and not that reproduced facing page 227 (and on p.viii of the Preface of this present volume). See W.Carruthers, 'On the Genuine and Spurious Portraits of Knox' in *United Free Church Magazine* (May 1906), 16-21. See also J.Drummond, 'Notes upon some Scottish Historical Portraits - John Knox' in *Proceedings of the Society of Antiquaries of Scotland* (1876) **11**:237-264.

[75] McCrie 120.   [76] McCrie 43.

[77] Ridley 103. See D.Guthrie, *History of Medicine* (London: Thomas Nelson, 1945), 169-171. Also page 44 of this present volume.

[78] Works **3**:167, note 2(A Godly Letter to the Faithfull in London, Newcastle & Berwick, 1554).

[79] Works **6**:77 (Letter XXXIV: Knox to Mrs Locke from St Andrews 2 September 1559). See also McCrie 173 and Mason 259-261.

[80] Works **3**:90. A Confession and Declaration of Prayer dated in the month of July 1554; Works **3**:364 (Letter XI: Knox to Mrs Bowes from Newcastle, 23 March 1553). See also McCrie 59; Ridley 152.

[81] Works **3**:351 (Letter IV: Knox to Mrs Bowes from Newcastle during 1553).

[82] Reid 75.

[83] F.A.MacCunn, *John Knox* (London: Methuen 1895), 13.

[84] J.Wilkinson, 'The Medical History of Martin Luther' in *Proc of R Coll Physicians Edinb* (1996) **26**:125. See pages 26-28 of this present volume.

[85] *Johannes Calvini Opera* (Brunswick: Schwelschke, 1863-1900) **20**: col. 34, letter 3961 (Calvin to Margaret, Queen of Navarre, 1 June 1563). This letter was written in French.

[86] Works **2**:403-421; Dickinson **2**:93-100.

[87] Works **3**:364 (Letter XI: Knox to Mrs Bowes from Newcastle 23 March 1553). Knox always regarded himself as a preacher rather than a writer. The result was that, in contrast to Luther and Calvin, he wrote and published no

commentaries on the books of the Bible. See Works **6**:229 (Preface by Knox to A Sermon on Isaiah 26:13-21 preached in St Giles, Edinburgh on Sunday 19 August 1565). This sermon is the only complete sermon we have from Knox's own pen, although it was written out by him from memory some thirteen days later. It was preached before Lord Henry Darnley whom Mary Queen of Scots had married on 29 July, and had been proclaimed as King of Scotland on the same day (Ridley 439).

[88] Works **6**:77 (Letter XXXIV: Knox to Mrs Locke from St Andrews, 2 September 1559). See McCrie 173.

[89] Works **6**:88 (Letter XXXVIII: Knox to Gregory Raylton from Edinburgh, midnight of 23 October 1559).

[90] Ridley 105.

[91] Brown **1**:151.

[92] Brown **2**:253.

[93] Bannatyne 62; McCrie 314. The word *resolution* used by Bannatyne is from the Latin verb *resoluo*, to loosen, which in medical authors was used to denote paralysis. See Celsus, *De Medicina* **3**:27,1A (Loeb edition **1**:345).

[94] Works **6**:479. Title page to 'An Answer to the Letter of James Tyrie, a Scottish Jesuit'.

[95] Bannatyne 62.   [96] McCrie, *Icones* 230.   [97] McCrie 333.

[98] Works **6**:569 (Letter LXXXVIII: Knox to Sir William Cecil from Edinburgh, 2 January 1569).

[99] Works **6**:482 (Preface to An Answer to the Letter of James Tyrie, a Scottish Jesuit, 1572). Cp Ref. 111 below.

[100] Works **6**:616 (Letter CI: Knox to Sir James Douglas of Drumlanrig from St Andrews, 26 May 1572). See also Brown **2**:274.

[101] Works **6**:lv (Knox's Last Will and Testament). See also McCrie 499.

[102] Bannatyne 62; McCrie 319.

[103] Melville 26; Brown **2**:266, note 1. 'So far was it from being true, as is commonly asserted, that he had caused the destruction of the abbey and the abbey church or cathedral in 1559, that in 1571 he found a habitable building there in which he, a frail old man, with his wife and children, could pass the winter in comfort'. See A.F.Mitchell, *The Scottish Reformation* (Edinburgh: William Blackwood & Sons, 1900), 192.

[104] Works **6**:604-605 (Letter XCVII: Knox to the General Assembly at Stirling from St Andrews, 3 August 1571).

[105] Bannatyne 255; Melville 21.

[106] R.Pitcairn (ed), *The Autobiography and Diary of Mr James Melville* (Edinburgh: The Wodrow Society, 1842), i-lxiv. This is a short biography of Melville written by the editor and prefixed to the book.

[107] Melville 26; Dickinson **1**:lxvi.

[108] Melville 21.   [109] See Reference 100 above.

[110] Dickinson **1**:lxvi-lxvii; Works **6**:617 (Letter CII: Knox to Sir John Wishart of Pittarrow from St Andrews, 19 July 1572).

[111] Works **6**:473-520 (An Answer to a Letter written by James Tyrie, A Scottish Jesuit, 1572).

[112] This house is on the north side of the High Street about a quarter of a mile down from St Giles. It was allocated to Knox by the Town Council which was responsible for his accommodation. Its owner was Sir James Mosman (or Mossman), a goldsmith, whose father had made the crown for Mary of Guise-Lorraine when she became the queen of James V in 1538. Mosman, being a supporter of Mary, Queen of Scots, had removed to the security of the Castle in April 1572, leaving the house at the disposal of the Council when he was outlawed and his possessions became forfeit. See Brown **2**:315-319; Cowan 383-390 and also D.Smith, *John Knox House: Gateway to Edinburgh's Old Town* (Edinburgh: John Donald, 1996).

[113] Bannatyne 263. See J.C.Lees, *St Giles', Edinburgh: Church, College, & Cathedral* (Edinburgh: W & R Chambers, 1889), 157-158 and A.I.Dunlop, *The Kirks of Edinburgh 1560-1984* (Edinburgh: Scottish Record Society, 1988) 15. See also Works **6**:631, note 2.

[114] Works **6**:633 (Letter CVIII: Sir Henry Killigrew to Lord Burghley (William Cecil) and Robert, Earl of Leicester, from Edinburgh dated 6 October 1572).

[115] Smeton 654; McCrie 337-338; Ridley 515.

[116] The last days of the life of Knox are described on pages 281 to 289 of Bannatyne's *Memorials*. This section of the Memorials was published separately in an annotated edition with modernised spelling by David Hay Fleming (Edinburgh: The Knox Club, 1913).

[117] Bannatyne 281; Smeton 654. Smeton speaks of 'a continual defluxion' or flow of phlegm, which obstructed Knox's air passages and made his breathing difficult. Smeton also gives the date on which this fit of severe coughing occurred as Monday 10 November.

[118] Smeton 654.

[119] Bannatyne 285; McCrie 342.

[120] Bannatyne 287; Smeton 658.

[121] Smeton 658.

[122] *Ibidem*.

[123] Bannatyne 288; Smeton 659.

[124] Bannatyne 289; McCrie 346.

[125] Melville 84. Melville notes that Morton's speech was laconic even on the scaffold. See also Bannatyne 331.

[126] Melville 47; Bannatyne 290; Brown **2**:288, note 2. See also the fuller record of Morton's testimony to Knox in Calderwood **3**:242, quoted in Works **6**:lii.

[127] Pearce GR. *John Knox* (London: Duckworth, 1936), 139.

[128] Bannatyne 281; Smeton 654.   [129] Bannatyne 285; McCrie 342.

[130] Smeton 641-642.   [131] Bannatyne 288; Smeton 658.

[132] Smeton 654.   [133] Bannatyne 285.

[134] McCrie, *Icones* 231.

INDEX